Make a Million Dollar

Unleash the Power o

Anjelica Shaw

MAKE A MILLION DOLLARS WITH MAGICK: UNLEASH THE POWER OF ABUNDANCE

First edition. August 12, 2023.

Copyright © 2023 Anjelica Shaw.

ISBN: 979-8223514442

Written by Anjelica Shaw.

Table of Contents

In the boundless realm of possibilities, where the mystical and the practical converge, lies a transformative path to financial prosperity like no other. Welcome to the extraordinary world of "Make a Million Dollars with Magick," where the art of financial manifestation and the esoteric powers of magick entwine to unlock the doors to unimaginable abundance. Within these pages, you will embark on a journey that transcends conventional wealth-building strategies, revealing the secrets of harnessing intention, visualization, and universal energy to make your million-dollar dreams a reality. Prepare to awaken the magick within you, as we delve deep into the sacred teachings, empowering rituals, and potent spells that will pave your way to financial opulence. Get ready to step beyond the confines of ordinary reality and embrace the extraordinary, for the key to a million-dollar fortune awaits, and it is magickal.

Chapter 1: Introduction

This chapter sets the foundation for understanding the role of magick in achieving financial abundance. It emphasizes the importance of having the right money mindset and the power of intention and the Law of Attraction. You will learn about the significance of money visualization and how to cultivate an abundance mindset.

1.1 The Magick of Financial Abundance

Welcome to the world of financial magick, where the ancient wisdom of metaphysics meets the modern pursuit of prosperity. In this chapter, we embark on a journey to explore the profound connection between magick and financial abundance. Magick, as we refer to it here, is not about conjuring illusions or trickery but harnessing the hidden forces of the universe to align with your financial aspirations. It is a path of empowerment that invites you to become the master of your financial destiny.

1.2 Your Money Mindset Matters

Before delving into the intricacies of financial magick, it is crucial to address the foundation on which it stands: your money mindset. Your beliefs, attitudes, and feelings about money shape your financial reality. If you harbor limiting beliefs about wealth or fear financial success, it becomes challenging to manifest abundance.

This chapter encourages you to reflect on your current money mindset and recognize any negative thought patterns that may hinder your financial growth. By identifying and releasing these limiting beliefs, you make room for a new and empowering perspective on money—one that aligns with the principles of financial magick.

1.3 Unleashing the Power of Intention

At the heart of all magick lies intention—a clear and focused desire that acts as the catalyst for manifestation. In the realm of financial magick, setting powerful intentions is essential to attract prosperity into your life. We explore how to craft effective intentions that are specific, positive, and aligned with your core values.

Understanding the mechanics of intention allows you to infuse your financial goals with a magickal charge, propelling them forward into the realm of possibility. By mastering the art of intention, you become the architect of your financial reality.

1.4 Embracing the Law of Attraction

The Law of Attraction, a fundamental principle of the universe, states that like attracts like. In the context of financial magick, this means that aligning your energy with the vibration of abundance attracts more wealth into your life. This chapter delves into the workings of the Law of Attraction and how it influences your financial experiences.

By becoming conscious of your thoughts, feelings, and actions, you can harmonize your energy with the frequency of prosperity. Learn how to attract opportunities, resources, and financial blessings through the magnetic power of your own consciousness.

1.5 The Magick of Money Visualization

Visualization is a potent tool in the practice of financial magick. By vividly imagining your desired financial reality, you create a blueprint for the universe to follow. In this chapter, we explore techniques to refine your visualization abilities, infusing them with clarity, emotion, and detail.

As you immerse yourself in the magickal realm of visualization, you begin to dissolve the barriers between your current financial circumstances and the abundance you seek. Embrace the power of your mind's eye to shape the contours of your financial destiny.

1.6 Cultivating an Abundance Mindset

To harness the full potential of financial magick, cultivating an abundance mindset is paramount. An abundance mindset transcends scarcity and fear, inviting you to perceive the limitless opportunities that surround you. In this concluding section of Chapter 1, we delve into practices and affirmations to nourish your abundance mindset.

By shifting your perspective from lack to abundance, you realign your consciousness with the natural flow of prosperity. With this newfound mindset and the knowledge gained in this chapter, you will be ready to embrace the transformative journey of financial magick. As you step forward, remember that the universe is conspiring to bring forth your greatest financial potential. Embrace the magick that lies within and watch as financial abundance unfolds before you.

1.2: Your Money Mindset Matters

In the realm of financial magick, your mind wields incredible power. Your thoughts, beliefs, and attitudes about money shape your financial reality, determining whether abundance flows effortlessly into your life or if you encounter persistent challenges. Before we delve deeper into the mysteries of financial magick, it is crucial to explore and transform your money mindset.

1. The Influence of Past Conditioning

Your money mindset is not an inherent trait but a product of conditioning. From a young age, you absorb beliefs about money from your family, society, and culture. These beliefs form the foundation of your financial beliefs and behaviors, often operating beneath the surface of your awareness.

Take some time for introspection and reflection to uncover the beliefs that influence your relationship with money. Are you holding onto limiting beliefs about scarcity or unworthiness? Do you associate money with negative emotions or feel guilty about desiring wealth? Identifying these patterns is the first step in releasing their hold on your financial journey.

2. Recognizing and Releasing Limiting Beliefs

Once you have identified your limiting beliefs, it is time to release them and make space for new empowering beliefs. Challenge the validity of old beliefs and question their origins. Remember that you have the power to create your reality, and limiting beliefs only serve to hold you back from your true potential.

Affirmations, journaling, and meditation are powerful tools to aid in this process. Create positive affirmations that counteract your old limiting beliefs and repeat them daily to reprogram your subconscious mind. Journaling can help you explore the roots of your beliefs and release any emotional attachments to them. Meditation allows you to quiet the mind and connect with your inner wisdom, gaining clarity and insight into your money mindset.

3. Embracing an Abundance Mindset

As you shed old limiting beliefs, consciously adopt an abundance mindset—a state of mind where you believe in the limitless opportunities for financial growth and success. Embrace the idea that there is more than enough for everyone and that your financial prosperity does not diminish others.

An abundance mindset opens the door to creativity, innovation, and a willingness to take calculated risks. When you view money as a flowing energy, you attract opportunities and resources that align with your positive beliefs. Celebrate every financial win, no matter how small, and use it as evidence that abundance is manifesting in your life.

4. Gratitude as a Path to Abundance

Gratitude is a powerful practice that complements an abundance mindset. Cultivate a daily gratitude practice by acknowledging and appreciating the abundance you already have in your life. When you focus on what you are grateful for, you shift your attention away from lack and scarcity, thereby inviting more blessings into your life.

Express gratitude for the money you have, the opportunities you encounter, and the progress you make on your financial journey. Gratitude acts as a magnet, drawing in more reasons to be thankful and amplifying your abundance.

5. The Power of Positive Affirmations

Positive affirmations are potent tools to reinforce your abundance mindset. Craft affirmations that reflect the financial reality you desire. For example, say, "I am a magnet for financial abundance," "I attract prosperity effortlessly," or "Money flows to me from unexpected sources."

Repeat these affirmations with conviction and emotion, allowing them to sink deep into your subconscious mind. As you consistently affirm your financial success, you align your energy with the vibration of abundance and draw it into your life.

Conclusion:

Your money mindset matters more than you may realize. It serves as the foundation on which you build your financial reality. By recognizing and transforming limiting beliefs, embracing an abundance mindset, practicing gratitude, and using positive affirmations, you can pave the way for a magickal journey to financial abundance.

Remember, you have the power to rewrite your money story and manifest the prosperity you deserve. With a liberated and empowered money mindset, you become the architect of your financial destiny, shaping a life of abundance and fulfillment. As you continue your exploration of financial magick, keep these transformative principles at the forefront of your mind, knowing that they hold the key to unlocking the full potential of your financial magick journey.

1.3: Unleashing the Power of Intention

Intention is the spark that ignites the flames of manifestation in the world of financial magick. It is the focused desire that sets the wheels of abundance in motion, drawing opportunities, resources, and prosperity towards you. In this chapter, we delve into the profound significance of intention and explore how to harness its transformative power to manifest your financial dreams.

1. Understanding the Nature of Intention

At its core, intention is a conscious decision to bring a specific outcome into being. It is not merely a wish or a fleeting thought; instead, it is a deliberate and unwavering focus on what you truly desire in your financial life. By defining your intentions clearly, you give direction to the magickal forces that conspire to support you.

In financial magick, intention acts as the driving force behind every spell, ritual, or action you undertake. It is the guiding star that leads you towards your financial goals. Embrace the realization that you possess the power to shape your financial reality through the deliberate use of intention.

2. Crafting Effective Intentions

To wield the power of intention effectively, it is essential to craft intentions that are both specific and positive. Vague or negatively framed intentions can lead to ambiguous outcomes or unintended consequences. Be clear about what you want to manifest and ensure that your intentions are aligned with your highest good and the greater good of all.

For instance, instead of setting an intention like, "I don't want to be in debt anymore," reframe it to a positive and specific intention like, "I am financially free and experience abundance in all aspects of my life."

3. Aligning Intention with Core Values

Intention gains strength when it aligns with your core values and authentic desires. Reflect on what truly matters to you in your financial journey. Is it financial freedom, the ability to contribute to causes you care about, or the capacity to provide for your loved ones? Connecting your intentions with your deepest values infuses your magick with passion and purpose.

4. Charging Your Intentions with Emotion

Emotion is the fuel that powers intention in the world of magick. When you infuse your intentions with genuine emotion, you amplify their magickal potency. Feel the excitement, joy, and gratitude as you envision your financial goals coming to fruition. This emotional charge sends a clear and powerful message to the universe, signaling your unwavering commitment to your intentions.

5. The Power of Rituals in Reinforcing Intentions

Rituals are magickal acts that serve to solidify and intensify your intentions. By creating a sacred space, incorporating symbols, and following a ceremonial structure, rituals elevate your intentions to a higher frequency. Whether it's a simple candle lighting ceremony or a complex ritual, the act of performing a magickal ceremony enhances the focus and energy behind your intentions.

6. Surrendering and Trusting the Universe

While setting powerful intentions is essential, it is equally important to surrender the outcome to the universe and trust the magickal process. Resistance or doubt can create energetic barriers that hinder the flow of abundance. Release any attachment to how and when your intentions will manifest, and have faith that the universe is conspiring in your favor.

Conclusion:

In the realm of financial magick, intention is the catalyst that activates the forces of manifestation. By understanding the nature of intention, crafting clear and positive intentions aligned with your core values, charging them with authentic emotion, and reinforcing them through rituals, you unleash the true power of intention in your financial journey.

With intention as your guiding force, you take control of your financial destiny, shaping a reality where abundance and prosperity are drawn to you effortlessly. Embrace the transformative potential of intention as you embark on your magickal journey to financial abundance, knowing that the universe is ready to support your every step towards prosperity.

1.4: Embracing the Law of Attraction

In the realm of financial magick, the Law of Attraction is a fundamental principle that governs the manifestation of abundance. It asserts that like attracts like and that the energy you emit into the universe shapes your reality. Embracing the Law of Attraction empowers you to become a conscious creator of your financial destiny. In this chapter, we explore the intricacies of this universal law and discover how to harness its transformative potential to attract financial prosperity.

1. The Law of Attraction: A Universal Principle

The Law of Attraction is not a magical incantation or a mystical concept; it is a natural law that operates universally. It states that similar energies attract each other, meaning that positive or negative thoughts and emotions attract corresponding experiences into your life.

Understanding this law is crucial to your financial magick journey. By aligning your thoughts, emotions, and actions with the frequency of abundance, you create a magnetic field that draws prosperity and financial opportunities towards you.

2. The Power of Thoughts and Beliefs

Thoughts are the building blocks of your reality. Your beliefs and perceptions about money act as powerful magnets that shape your financial experiences. If you hold onto limiting beliefs about scarcity or doubt your ability to achieve financial success, you unknowingly repel abundance.

Conversely, by cultivating positive thoughts and empowering beliefs about money, you align your energy with the frequency of abundance. Embrace a mindset that welcomes financial prosperity, believing in your capacity to manifest wealth and attract opportunities for growth.

3. The Role of Emotions in Attraction

Emotions are energetic signatures that intensify the Law of Attraction. When you experience emotions such as joy, gratitude, and enthusiasm, you radiate positive vibrations into the universe. These high-frequency emotions act as powerful beacons that draw positive experiences and financial blessings into your life.

On the other hand, negative emotions like fear, doubt, and envy can create barriers to abundance. Recognize and process any negative emotions around money, transforming them into positive and constructive energies that support your financial goals.

4. Visualization and Feeling as Tools of Attraction

Visualization is a potent tool for harnessing the Law of Attraction in financial magick. By vividly imagining your financial success and feeling the emotions associated with achievement, you create a powerful magnet for prosperity. Visualization aligns your subconscious mind with your desires, imprinting them into the fabric of your reality.

Consistently engage in visualization exercises, allowing yourself to feel the excitement and fulfillment that accompany financial abundance. Embrace this as your new reality, knowing that the universe is receptive to your magnetic intentions.

5. Taking Inspired Action

While the Law of Attraction is a powerful force, it is essential to remember that it is not a passive process. Taking inspired action is a crucial aspect of aligning with abundance. Opportunities and synchronicities often arise as a result of your actions, signaling that the universe is responding to your intentions.

Pay attention to intuitive nudges and seize opportunities that align with your financial goals. Trust your inner guidance and step confidently into the path of your financial dreams, knowing that the Law of Attraction supports your efforts.

6. Gratitude as an Amplifier of Attraction

Gratitude is the master amplifier of the Law of Attraction. By expressing genuine gratitude for the abundance in your life, you signal to the universe that you are open to receiving more blessings. Gratitude raises your vibration and expands your capacity to attract greater financial prosperity.

Cultivate a daily gratitude practice, acknowledging all the ways in which abundance manifests in your life. As you embrace a grateful heart, you become a magnet for even more reasons to be thankful.

Conclusion:

The Law of Attraction is a guiding principle in the realm of financial magick. By consciously aligning your thoughts, beliefs, emotions, and actions with the frequency of abundance, you attract prosperity and financial opportunities into your life. Embrace the power of your mind and emotions as tools of attraction, and let gratitude be the magnetic force that amplifies your financial blessings.

As you fully embrace the Law of Attraction on your magickal journey to financial abundance, remember that you are a co-creator of your reality. Harness this universal law to shape a financial destiny that reflects your deepest desires and supports your highest good. The universe eagerly awaits your magnetic intentions, ready to unfold a path of prosperity and fulfillment before you.

1.5: The Magick of Money Visualization

Visualization is a powerful technique that bridges the gap between imagination and manifestation. In the realm of financial magick, money visualization serves as a potent tool to bring your financial goals to life and align your consciousness with the frequency of abundance. In this chapter, we explore the transformative magick of money visualization and how to master this practice to attract wealth and prosperity.

1. The Creative Power of the Mind

The mind is a vast landscape where thoughts and images take form. Visualization taps into the mind's creative power, allowing you to vividly imagine your financial desires as if they were already manifesting. When you create a mental image of your financial success, you stimulate the same neural pathways as if you were experiencing it in reality, sending a powerful signal to the universe.

2. Creating Detailed and Sensory-Rich Visualizations

To maximize the impact of money visualization, infuse your mental images with rich sensory details. Imagine the sights, sounds, smells, and feelings associated with your financial success. Visualize the gleam of money, the excitement of achieving your financial goals, and the sense of security and abundance that accompanies prosperity.

The more vivid and emotionally charged your visualizations are, the more they resonate with the universe, magnetizing your desires towards you.

3. The Art of Emotional Alignment

Emotion is the fuel that ignites the magick of money visualization. As you immerse yourself in your financial dreams, feel the genuine excitement, joy, and gratitude for your achievements. Embrace the emotions that align with financial abundance, as they amplify the magnetic power of your visualizations.

Remember that your emotional state serves as a barometer for your alignment with your intentions. If you encounter feelings of doubt or resistance during your visualizations, acknowledge them without judgment, and gently guide your focus back to positive emotions of abundance.

4. Consistency and Repetition

Like any magickal practice, money visualization requires consistency and repetition to yield significant results. Set aside dedicated time each day to engage in your visualizations. Treat this practice as a sacred ritual, where you connect deeply with your financial desires and emotions.

As you repeat your visualizations regularly, you strengthen the energetic imprint of your financial goals in your subconscious mind and the collective consciousness, paving the way for their manifestation.

5. Letting Go and Surrendering

While visualization is a powerful technique, it is equally important to surrender the how and when of your financial desires to the universe. Trust that the magickal process is at work, orchestrating events and synchronicities to bring your intentions to fruition.

Let go of any attachment to the outcome and maintain an attitude of trust and openness. Allow the universe to surprise you with unexpected opportunities and blessings that align with your financial goals.

6. Gratitude as an Amplifier

Gratitude is an essential aspect of money visualization. As you visualize your financial success, infuse your practice with heartfelt gratitude for the abundance that is already present in your life. This gratitude amplifies the magnetic power of your visualizations and invites even more prosperity into your reality.

Conclusion:

The magick of money visualization is a transformative practice that empowers you to co-create your financial reality. Through the creative power of your mind and the depth of your emotions, you shape a magnetic field that attracts wealth and abundance.

Master the art of money visualization by creating sensory-rich and emotionally charged mental images, engaging in consistent and repetitive practice, and surrendering the outcome to the universe with trust and gratitude. Embrace this magickal tool on your journey to financial abundance, knowing that the universe eagerly supports your intentions and stands ready to manifest your financial dreams into reality.

1.6: Cultivating an Abundance Mindset

In the world of financial magick, the abundance mindset is a transformative state of consciousness that acts as a fertile ground for prosperity to flourish. Cultivating an abundance mindset goes beyond a mere positive attitude; it is a deep-seated belief in the limitless possibilities of financial success and the unwavering trust in the abundance that surrounds us. In this chapter, we explore the principles and practices to cultivate an abundance mindset and open the floodgates to financial prosperity.

1. Embracing the Abundance Paradigm

The abundance paradigm is a shift in perception that moves you away from scarcity and lack towards recognizing the boundless opportunities for financial growth. In an abundant universe, there is more than enough for everyone, and your financial success does not diminish that of others. Embrace the belief that the universe is a generous provider and that abundance is your birthright.

2. Releasing Limiting Beliefs of Scarcity

To embrace an abundance mindset, it is crucial to release limiting beliefs of scarcity that may have been ingrained in your consciousness. Let go of thoughts like "money is hard to come by," "there is not enough to go around," or "wealth is only for the lucky few." Replace these beliefs with empowering affirmations that affirm your deservingness of financial abundance.

3. Gratitude as the Gateway to Abundance

Gratitude is a powerful practice that acts as a key to unlocking the doors of abundance. Cultivate a daily gratitude ritual, where you acknowledge and appreciate the abundance already present in your life. By focusing on what you have rather than what you lack, you shift your perspective towards abundance and attract even more reasons to be thankful.

4. Embodying the Frequency of Abundance

An abundance mindset is not merely a mental exercise; it is an embodiment of the frequency of abundance. Align your thoughts, emotions, and actions with the vibration of prosperity. Act as if you are already living in a state of financial abundance, and let this energy ripple out into the universe.

Be generous with your time, resources, and compliments, knowing that the more you give, the more you receive. Embrace an attitude of openness and receptivity to financial blessings, trusting that the universe is conspiring in your favor.

5. The Power of Affirmations and Afformations

Affirmations are positive statements that reinforce your abundance mindset. Craft empowering affirmations that reflect your financial aspirations and repeat them daily to rewire your subconscious mind.

Afformations, on the other hand, are questions that focus your mind on positive outcomes. For instance, instead of saying, "I am financially abundant," ask yourself, "Why am I so financially successful?" This subtle shift in language directs your mind towards seeking positive evidence, further cementing your abundance mindset.

6. Embracing Abundance Mentors

Surround yourself with individuals who embody the abundance mindset. Seek out mentors, role models, or like-minded individuals who have achieved financial success and are willing to share their wisdom and experiences.

Learning from those who have already cultivated an abundance mindset can offer valuable insights and inspiration on your own journey towards financial prosperity.

Conclusion:

Cultivating an abundance mindset is a transformative practice that empowers you to step into the flow of financial abundance. Embrace the principles of the abundance paradigm, release limiting beliefs of scarcity, and immerse yourself in the practice of gratitude. Align your thoughts, emotions, and actions with the frequency of abundance, and reinforce your mindset with empowering affirmations and afformations.

As you embrace the energy of abundance, you open yourself to the magickal currents that attract wealth and prosperity into your life. Trust that the universe is infinitely abundant and that by embracing this truth, you step into the realm of limitless financial possibilities. Embrace the abundance mindset as the foundation of your financial magick journey, knowing that you are a co-creator of your prosperous reality.

1.7: Practical Exercises for Chapter 1

1.1 The Magick of Financial Abundance:

Exercise 1: Gratitude Journal

Start a gratitude journal dedicated to your financial journey. Each day, write down at least three things you are grateful for regarding money and finances. It could be receiving unexpected money, having a stable job, or even having the ability to pay bills. Cultivating gratitude for your current financial situation sets the stage for attracting more abundance into your life.

1.2 Your Money Mindset Matters:

Exercise 2: Identify and Challenge Limiting Beliefs

Take some time for introspection and identify any limiting beliefs you have about money and wealth. Write them down in a journal. Next, challenge these beliefs by asking yourself if they are based on facts or just conditioned thoughts. Replace each limiting belief with a positive affirmation that supports an empowering money mindset. For example, if you have the belief "Money is evil," replace it with "Money is a tool for good in my life and the lives of others."

1.3 Unleashing the Power of Intention:

Exercise 3: Craft Specific Financial Intentions

Spend time in a quiet space where you can focus. Write down your financial intentions as clearly and specifically as possible. Be detailed about the financial goals you want to achieve, such as paying off debts, saving a certain amount of money, or starting a new venture. Visualize yourself achieving these goals with excitement and confidence.

1.4 Embracing the Law of Attraction:

Exercise 4: Positive Thought Awareness

Throughout the day, be mindful of your thoughts and feelings about money. Whenever you catch yourself thinking negatively or with doubt about your financial situation, consciously replace those thoughts with positive ones. Focus on affirmations like "I am a magnet for financial abundance" or "I attract wealth and opportunities effortlessly."

1.5 The Magick of Money Visualization:

Exercise 5: Daily Visualization Practice

Set aside 10-15 minutes each day for money visualization. Sit comfortably in a quiet space, close your eyes, and visualize your financial goals coming to fruition. Use all your senses to make the visualization as vivid as possible. Feel the joy, excitement, and gratitude as you see yourself achieving your financial dreams.

1.6 Cultivating an Abundance Mindset:

Exercise 6: Abundance Afformations

Create a list of afformations that focus on abundance and prosperity. Ask yourself questions like "Why am I so financially successful?" or "Why do opportunities for wealth flow to me effortlessly?" Repeat these afformations throughout the day, engaging your mind to seek positive evidence of your financial success.

Exercise 7: Surround Yourself with Abundance Mentors

Identify individuals who embody the abundance mindset and have achieved financial success. Seek out their books, videos, or podcasts, and immerse yourself in their wisdom. Engage in conversations with like-minded individuals who are also on a journey towards financial abundance. Surrounding yourself with abundance mentors and positive influences will support your mindset transformation.

The practical exercises in this chapter are designed to empower you to embrace the magick of financial abundance. Through gratitude, challenging limiting beliefs, setting powerful intentions, cultivating positive thoughts, visualizing your financial success, and immersing yourself in an abundance mindset, you will activate the forces of manifestation in your financial journey. Commit to integrating these exercises into your daily routine and observe how your financial reality aligns with your empowered mindset. Remember, the universe is ready to support your journey towards prosperity and financial fulfillment.

Chapter 1 Conclusion:

In this introductory chapter, we have embarked on a transformative journey into the world of financial magick. We explored the profound connection between our mindset, intentions, and the universal forces that shape our financial reality. By embracing the principles of financial magick, we open ourselves to the unlimited possibilities of prosperity and abundance.

We began by understanding the significance of our money mindset—the beliefs and attitudes that govern our financial experiences. Through self-reflection and releasing limiting beliefs, we paved the way for a new and empowering perspective on money—one that aligns with the principles of financial magick.

Unleashing the power of intention, we discovered that it is the driving force that propels our financial aspirations into manifestation. By crafting specific and positive intentions and charging them with authentic emotion, we activated the magickal currents that draw opportunities and abundance towards us.

Embracing the Law of Attraction, we harnessed the universal principle that like attracts like. By aligning our thoughts, emotions, and actions with the frequency of abundance, we transformed ourselves into conscious creators of our financial destiny.

Through the magick of money visualization, we bridged the gap between imagination and reality, bringing our financial goals to life and immersing ourselves in the emotions of prosperity. By consistently engaging in this practice, we strengthened our connection to the magickal flow of abundance.

Cultivating an abundance mindset became the cornerstone of our financial magick journey. By embracing the abundance paradigm, releasing limiting beliefs, practicing gratitude, and aligning with the frequency of prosperity, we embodied the truth that abundance is our birthright.

As we conclude this chapter, remember that you are a powerful magickal being with the ability to manifest your financial dreams into reality. Embrace the practices and principles explored here, integrating them into your daily life. Embrace the magickal journey to financial abundance with an open heart and a willingness to co-create with the universe.

As we continue our exploration in the subsequent chapters, know that the path to financial magick is both empowering and transformative. Trust in the process, surrender the how and when, and stay open to the magickal opportunities that the universe presents.

Embrace your innate magick, and let it guide you towards a life of financial prosperity and fulfillment. As we move forward, remember that you are the master of your financial destiny, and the universe conspires to support you in every step of your magickal journey to financial abundance.

Chapter 2: The Elemental Foundations of Financial Magick

This chapter explores the connection between the elements (Earth, Air, Fire, Water, and Spirit) and financial success. Each element is associated with specific attributes that can be harnessed to support financial intentions. You will learn how to ground your financial goals, gain intellectual clarity, ignite passion, embrace emotional intelligence, and connect with universal abundance.

2.1: Earth: Grounding Your Financial Intentions

In the realm of financial magick, the elements serve as powerful archetypes that provide a profound understanding of the forces at play in our financial lives. Earth, as one of the foundational elements, represents stability, grounding, and material abundance. In this chapter, we explore the magickal significance of Earth and how to harness its energy to ground our financial intentions and manifest material prosperity.

1. Connecting with the Element of Earth

Earth is the element that anchors us to the physical realm, providing a stable foundation for our financial endeavors. To connect with the energy of Earth, spend time in nature, such as walking barefoot on the ground, gardening, or simply sitting in a park. Allow yourself to absorb the nurturing and grounding qualities of the Earth element, fostering a sense of stability and security in your financial pursuits.

2. Cultivating Material Abundance

In financial magick, Earth symbolizes material abundance and the manifestation of our financial goals in the physical world. To cultivate material abundance, align your financial intentions with the Earth element. Set realistic and achievable financial goals, taking practical steps towards their fulfillment. Just as a seed needs proper nourishment to grow, tend to your financial goals with diligence and consistency.

3. Creating an Abundance Altar

An abundance altar dedicated to the Earth element can be a focal point for your financial magick rituals. Decorate the altar with symbols of prosperity, such as green candles, crystals like citrine or pyrite, and coins or bills to represent material wealth. Offerings of fruits and herbs associated with abundance, such as basil or cinnamon, can be placed on the altar as a gesture of gratitude.

4. Grounding Your Financial Intentions

Before embarking on any financial magick or making significant financial decisions, ground yourself in the energy of Earth. Find a quiet space, sit or stand with your feet firmly on the ground, and take a few deep breaths. Imagine roots extending from the soles of your feet, burrowing deep into the Earth, anchoring you to its stability and support. Visualize the Earth's energy rising through your body, infusing your financial intentions with grounded strength and practicality.

5. The Magick of Abundance Crystals

Crystals associated with the Earth element can enhance your financial magick practices. Use crystals like green aventurine, tiger's eye, or jade in your abundance rituals and meditation sessions. Hold the crystal in your hand while visualizing your financial goals, allowing its energies to amplify your intentions and attract material prosperity.

Conclusion:

The Earth element forms a solid and dependable foundation for our financial magick journey. By connecting with the nurturing and grounding qualities of Earth, we cultivate material abundance and stability in our financial endeavors.

As we delve deeper into the elemental foundations of financial magick, remember that each element brings its unique energies and attributes. In the subsequent chapters, we will explore how to harness the powers of Air, Fire, Water, and Spirit to further enrich our financial magick practice.

Embrace the energy of Earth in grounding your financial intentions, and know that you have the power to manifest material prosperity in your life. As you continue your magickal journey towards financial abundance, let the wisdom of the Earth element guide you and support your quest for stability and prosperity.

2.2: Air: Intellectual Clarity and Wisdom in Money Matters

The element of Air represents the realm of intellect, communication, and mental clarity. In the context of financial magick, Air plays a crucial role in enhancing our understanding of money matters and making informed decisions. In this chapter, we explore the magickal significance of Air and how to harness its energy to gain intellectual clarity and wisdom in our financial pursuits.

1. Embracing the Element of Air

Air is the element that stimulates our mental faculties, enabling us to analyze, strategize, and communicate effectively. To connect with the energy of Air, spend time in open spaces with fresh air, practice deep breathing exercises, or engage in activities that encourage clear thinking, such as journaling or meditation. By embracing the essence of Air, we open the channels of intellectual insight and wisdom in our financial endeavors.

2. Cultivating Intellectual Clarity

In the realm of finances, intellectual clarity is essential for making sound decisions and planning for the future. Engage in activities that sharpen your mind, such as reading financial literature, attending workshops or seminars on money management, and seeking advice from financial experts. Cultivate the habit of researching and staying informed about financial trends and opportunities.

3. Harnessing the Power of Critical Thinking

Air is associated with critical thinking, which is vital for evaluating financial options and avoiding impulsive decisions. When faced with financial choices, take the time to analyze the pros and cons, consider potential risks, and assess the long-term implications. Critical thinking allows you to make informed choices that align with your financial goals.

4. Effective Communication in Financial Matters

Communication is another facet of Air's influence. Skillful communication about money matters is essential for partnerships, negotiations, and financial planning. Improve your ability to articulate your financial goals and boundaries clearly. Practice active listening to better understand the financial perspectives of others. Effective communication enhances collaboration and paves the way for financial success.

5. The Magick of Air Incense and Smudging

Air is closely linked to the power of scent. Use air-related practices like burning air-associated incense, such as lavender or frankincense, to create a calming and clear atmosphere during your financial magick rituals. Smudging with sage or palo santo can help dispel any mental clutter and create a space conducive to gaining intellectual clarity.

6. Seeking Guidance from the Higher Mind

Meditation is a potent tool for connecting with the higher mind and gaining wisdom in money matters. Set aside time for quiet contemplation, allowing your mind to become still and receptive to intuitive insights. Seek guidance from your higher self or spiritual guides regarding financial decisions, trusting that the answers will come when you are in a state of mental clarity.

Conclusion:

The element of Air serves as a guiding force in financial magick, bestowing us with intellectual clarity and wisdom in money matters. By embracing the essence of Air, cultivating critical thinking, and enhancing communication skills, we sharpen our financial acumen and make informed choices aligned with our goals.

As we continue our exploration of the elemental foundations of financial magick, let the wisdom of Air be our ally in navigating the complexities of financial decision-making. In the subsequent chapters, we will delve deeper into the transformative energies of Fire, Water, and Spirit, further enriching our financial magick practice.

Embrace the power of Air to gain intellectual clarity and harness the wisdom needed for financial success. As you embark on your magickal journey towards prosperity, remember that the element of Air is here to guide your mind and enlighten your financial path.

2.3: Fire: Igniting Passion and Motivation for Financial Success

The element of Fire represents the transformative power of passion, motivation, and action. In the realm of financial magick, Fire serves as the driving force that ignites our ambitions and propels us towards financial success. In this chapter, we explore the magickal significance of Fire and how to harness its energy to fuel our passion and motivation in achieving our financial goals.

1. Embracing the Element of Fire

Fire symbolizes the essence of transformation, vitality, and willpower. To connect with the energy of Fire, spend time in the presence of flames, such as a campfire or candles. Feel the warmth and intensity of Fire's energy, allowing it to awaken your inner drive and determination.

2. Awakening Your Financial Passion

Passion is the spark that ignites our financial endeavors and keeps us dedicated to our goals. Reflect on what truly ignites your passion in the realm of finances. Is it building a successful business, investing in projects that align with your values, or creating financial security for your loved ones? Embrace your financial passion as a powerful force that fuels your journey towards prosperity.

3. Setting Your Financial Goals Ablaze

Write down your financial goals in detail and visualize them as burning flames of desire. See each goal clearly, envisioning the steps required to achieve them. As you do this, feel the intensity of Fire's energy propelling you towards their realization. Allow your financial goals to be imbued with the fiery determination that will keep you motivated on your path.

4. Taking Inspired Action

Fire is associated with action and willpower. Once your financial goals are set ablaze with passion, take inspired action towards their fulfillment. Break down your goals into smaller actionable steps and commit to making progress each day. Embrace challenges as opportunities for growth and transformation, knowing that the fire within you burns brightly with the determination to succeed.

5. Fire Rituals for Financial Empowerment

Performing fire rituals can intensify your financial magick practice. Light a red or gold candle, and as it burns, visualize any limiting beliefs or obstacles being consumed by the flames. Replace those energies with feelings of empowerment and confidence. Offer written affirmations or symbolic representations of your financial goals to the fire as a symbol of releasing them into the universe.

6. Fanning the Flames of Motivation

Stay connected to the fiery energy of motivation by regularly revisiting your financial goals and affirmations. Surround yourself with reminders of your passion and determination, such as vision boards or inspirational quotes. Engage in activities that ignite your enthusiasm for financial success, such as attending motivational seminars or networking events.

Conclusion:

The element of Fire ignites the flames of passion and motivation in our financial magick journey. By embracing the transformative power of Fire, setting our financial goals ablaze with passion, and taking inspired action, we become unstoppable forces in achieving our financial dreams.

As we continue to explore the elemental foundations of financial magick, let the energy of Fire serve as a constant source of empowerment and determination. In the subsequent chapters, we will delve deeper into the energies of Water and Spirit, further enriching our financial magick practice.

Embrace the fire within you, igniting your financial passion and determination. Trust in the transformative power of Fire as it fuels your journey towards financial success. As you walk this magickal path, know that you possess the power to make your financial dreams a blazing reality.

2.4: Water: Embracing Emotional Intelligence for Financial Well-Being

The element of Water symbolizes the realm of emotions, intuition, and adaptability. In the realm of financial magick, Water plays a crucial role in understanding and managing our emotional relationship with money. By embracing emotional intelligence, we create a harmonious flow that supports our financial well-being. In this chapter, we explore the magickal significance of Water and how to harness its energy to cultivate emotional intelligence for financial success.

1. Embracing the Element of Water

Water is a symbol of fluidity and adaptability. To connect with the energy of Water, spend time near bodies of water such as lakes, rivers, or the ocean. Observe the ever-changing nature of water and reflect on its ability to flow with ease. Allow the soothing energy of Water to inspire emotional balance and flexibility in your financial endeavors.

2. Understanding Your Emotional Relationship with Money

Reflect on your emotional relationship with money. How do you feel when you think about finances or when making financial decisions? Are there any emotional patterns or triggers that arise in money-related situations? By gaining insight into your emotional responses, you can cultivate emotional intelligence and make more conscious financial choices.

3. Cultivating Emotional Intelligence

Emotional intelligence involves recognizing and managing your emotions effectively. Practice self-awareness by acknowledging your feelings without judgment. Be honest with yourself about your financial fears, anxieties, or past money-related experiences that may be influencing your current beliefs and behaviors.

4. Healing Emotional Blocks

Water is a symbol of purification and cleansing. Use this element's energy to heal any emotional blocks or negative beliefs surrounding money. Engage in activities that promote emotional healing, such as journaling, meditation, or seeking support from a therapist or counselor.

5. Listening to Your Financial Intuition

Water is associated with intuition—the deep knowing that goes beyond logical reasoning. Trust your financial intuition when making decisions. If something doesn't feel right, take a step back and reevaluate. Similarly, if you feel a strong pull towards a particular opportunity, follow your intuition and explore it further.

6. Going with the Flow

Water teaches us the power of adaptability and going with the flow. Financial circumstances may change, and unexpected events can occur. Embrace the concept of adaptability in your financial journey, being open to new opportunities and adjusting your plans when necessary.

Conclusion:

The element of Water invites us to embrace emotional intelligence for financial well-being. By connecting with the fluidity of Water, understanding our emotional relationship with money, and cultivating emotional intelligence, we create a harmonious flow that supports our financial success.

As we continue to explore the elemental foundations of financial magick, let the energy of Water guide us in navigating the emotional aspects of money. In the subsequent chapters, we will delve deeper into the transformative energies of Spirit, further enriching our financial magick practice.

Embrace the power of Water, nurturing emotional intelligence for financial well-being. Trust in the intuitive wisdom of Water as it supports your financial journey. As you move forward, know that emotional balance and adaptability are your allies on this magickal path to financial abundance.

2.5: Spirit: Connecting with Universal Abundance

The element of Spirit represents the divine essence that permeates all of existence. It is the source of universal abundance and the interconnectedness of all things. In the realm of financial magick, connecting with the energy of Spirit opens us to the infinite possibilities of prosperity and aligns us with the flow of universal abundance. In this chapter, we explore the magickal significance of Spirit and how to harness its energy to establish a profound connection with universal abundance.

1. Embracing the Element of Spirit

Spirit is the element that transcends the physical realm and connects us to the divine. To connect with the energy of Spirit, engage in practices that foster a sense of spiritual connection, such as meditation, prayer, or spending time in nature. Embrace the understanding that you are a divine being, and your financial journey is part of the interconnected dance of universal abundance.

2. Recognizing Abundance as Your Birthright

Spirit reminds us that abundance is our birthright, and the universe is infinitely abundant. Release any feelings of unworthiness or scarcity, and affirm that you are deserving of all the abundance that life has to offer. Trust in the flow of universal abundance and know that it is always available to you.

3. Letting Go of Limiting Beliefs

Spirit invites us to release any limiting beliefs or blockages that hinder the flow of abundance. Engage in practices like journaling or meditation to identify and let go of beliefs that no longer serve your financial well-being. Replace these beliefs with empowering affirmations that align with the truth of universal abundance.

4. Surrendering to Divine Timing

Spirit teaches us the art of surrender—to trust that the universe has perfect timing for the manifestation of our financial goals. Practice patience and faith, knowing that the universe is orchestrating events to align with your highest good. Allow the magickal currents of Spirit to guide you towards the opportunities that will lead to financial abundance.

5. Gratitude as a Gateway to Spirit

Cultivate a deep sense of gratitude for the abundance already present in your life. Recognize that every breath, every experience, and every opportunity are gifts from the divine. Express heartfelt gratitude daily through prayer or meditation, inviting the presence of Spirit into your financial journey.

6. Aligning with the Flow of Universal Abundance

Spirit reminds us that we are co-creators with the universe. Set your intentions for financial success and then surrender them to the divine. Trust that the universe will respond to your desires in ways that exceed your expectations. Stay open and receptive to the signs and synchronicities that guide you towards the flow of universal abundance.

Conclusion:

The element of Spirit connects us to the infinite wellspring of universal abundance. By embracing the energy of Spirit, recognizing abundance as our birthright, and releasing limiting beliefs, we establish a profound connection with the flow of divine prosperity.

As we continue to explore the elemental foundations of financial magick, let the energy of Spirit be our guiding light on this magickal path. In the subsequent chapters, we will delve deeper into the transformative energies of Earth, Air, Fire, and Water, further enriching our financial magick practice.

Embrace the power of Spirit, connecting with universal abundance in your financial journey. Trust in the divine orchestration of your prosperity, knowing that you are a channel for the limitless flow of abundance from the universe.

As you walk this magickal path, remember that you are an integral part of the grand tapestry of universal abundance.

2.6: The Magickal Alchemy of Million-Dollar Ambitions

As we delve deeper into the elemental foundations of financial magick, a profound realization dawns upon us: the path to making a million dollars with magick is an alchemical journey of transformation and empowerment. With each element serving as a catalyst for financial growth, we uncover the magickal alchemy that leads us to our desired destination of abundance.

Earth, the grounding force, provides the solid foundation upon which our million-dollar ambitions rest. Like the roots of a mighty tree, our financial intentions take root in the fertile soil of practicality and steadfast determination. By grounding ourselves in the present moment and nurturing our financial goals with care, we ensure that they blossom into fruition.

Air, the realm of intellectual clarity and wisdom, becomes the vessel that carries our financial decisions towards success. By cultivating a clear vision and understanding of the opportunities that lay before us, we can make informed choices that steer us towards financial growth and prosperity.

Fire, the igniting force of passion and ambition, fans the flames of our million-dollar dreams. Like a blazing fire that fuels our drive, this element propels us forward with unwavering determination and unwavering focus. Embracing the fire within, we unleash our potential and set ablaze the path to our financial aspirations.

Water, the essence of emotional intelligence, teaches us to navigate the ebb and flow of financial challenges. By embracing emotional balance and resilience, we remain steadfast in the face of setbacks, allowing us to adapt, learn, and grow on our journey to a million dollars.

Spirit, the gateway to universal abundance, connects us to the infinite flow of prosperity. Through spiritual alignment and conscious co-creation with the cosmos, we open ourselves to receive the gifts of abundance that the universe graciously bestows upon us.

As the elemental forces converge, we witness the alchemical fusion of their energies, creating a powerful synergy that propels our financial manifestations towards the million-dollar mark. The practicality of earth combines with the wisdom of air, fueled by the passion of fire, and balanced by the emotional intelligence of water—all guided by the divine flow of spirit.

In this magickal alchemy, we discover that making a million dollars with magick is not solely about material gain but about embracing the transformation of our entire being. It is a journey of self-discovery, empowerment, and alignment with our highest potential.

As we harness the elemental forces within and without, we remember that the magickal journey to a million dollars is not instantaneous but a gradual process of growth and evolution. It requires patience, dedication, and unwavering belief in the power of magick to shape our reality.

With each step on this alchemical path, we move closer to the manifestation of a million-dollar fortune. Through the integration of the elemental forces in our financial magick, we cultivate a prosperous mindset, align ourselves with the universal flow of abundance, and make the million-dollar dream a tangible reality.

In this magickal dance of alchemy, the universe conspires to support our aspirations, and we become the master alchemists of our own destiny. With the wisdom of the elements as our guide, we step boldly into the realm of financial abundance, embracing the transformative power of magick to make a million dollars and unlock the infinite possibilities that lie ahead.

2.7: Practical Exercises for Chapter 2

2.1 Earth: Grounding Your Financial Intentions

Exercise 1: Earth Connection Meditation

Find a quiet and comfortable space. Close your eyes and take several deep breaths. Imagine roots extending from the soles of your feet, going deep into the Earth. Feel yourself becoming grounded and anchored to the Earth's stability. Visualize your financial intentions as seeds planted deep within the Earth. Envision them growing into strong and abundant manifestations. Spend a few minutes in this meditation daily to reinforce your connection to the Earth element and ground your financial intentions.

Exercise 2: Financial Vision Board

Create a financial vision board using Earth-related elements such as earthy colors, images of landscapes, and symbols of stability and growth. Include pictures that represent your financial goals and aspirations. Display your vision board in a prominent place where you can see it daily. The vision board will serve as a tangible reminder of your financial intentions and keep you focused on your path to prosperity.

2.2 Air: Intellectual Clarity and Wisdom in Money Matters

Exercise 3: Financial Journaling

Start a financial journal to explore your thoughts and feelings about money. Write about your beliefs, fears, and past experiences related to finances. Use this journal to brainstorm financial goals, strategies, and action plans. Regular journaling can enhance your financial clarity and provide insights into your relationship with money.

Exercise 4: Mind Mapping for Financial Decision-Making

Use mind mapping as a tool for decision-making in financial matters. When faced with significant financial choices, create a mind map by placing the decision in the center and branching out with the pros, cons, and potential outcomes. This exercise will help you see the bigger picture and make informed choices.

2.3 Fire: Igniting Passion and Motivation for Financial Success

Exercise 5: Passion Visualization

Sit in a quiet space, close your eyes, and take a few deep breaths. Visualize a flame in your heart center, representing your financial passion. See the flame grow brighter and stronger as you connect with your financial goals and desires. Feel the fire igniting your motivation and determination to achieve success. Embrace this visualization regularly to keep your financial passion alive.

Exercise 6: Action Plan Enchantment

Write down your financial goals on separate pieces of paper. Hold each paper over a lit candle (safely, without burning it) and infuse the goals with your passion and determination. As you do this, repeat empowering affirmations related to your financial success. The act of infusing your goals with fire energy will empower your commitment to taking inspired action.

2.4 Water: Embracing Emotional Intelligence for Financial Well-Being

Exercise 7: Emotional Release Ritual

Create a sacred space for emotional release. Light a blue candle and write down any negative emotions or limiting beliefs you have about money. Read each one aloud and, as you do, imagine releasing them into the flame. Visualize the emotional burdens dissipating, leaving you with a sense of emotional freedom and clarity.

Exercise 8: Gratitude Flow

Create a daily gratitude practice centered around your financial well-being. Before going to bed, write down at least three financial aspects or experiences for which you are grateful. Embrace feelings of appreciation and abundance as you express gratitude. This exercise will align your emotions with the flow of universal abundance.

2.5 Spirit: Connecting with Universal Abundance

Exercise 9: Abundance Affirmations

Craft powerful affirmations that affirm your connection to universal abundance. For example, "I am a channel of universal prosperity" or "I am open to receiving the abundance of the universe." Repeat these affirmations daily, engaging with the energy of Spirit and aligning yourself with the flow of abundance.

Exercise 10: Divine Guidance Meditation

Engage in a meditation to connect with the guidance of Spirit. Sit in a quiet space, breathe deeply, and invite divine wisdom and insights regarding your financial journey. Trust any intuitive messages or visions that come to you during this meditation. Connecting with Spirit in this way will deepen your understanding of your financial path.

The practical exercises in this chapter empower you to integrate the energies of Earth, Air, Fire, Water, and Spirit into your financial magick practice. By grounding your financial intentions, gaining intellectual clarity, igniting passion, embracing emotional intelligence, and connecting with universal abundance, you become a conscious creator of your financial reality.

As you continue to work with the elemental energies, remember that you are a magickal being with the power to manifest prosperity and abundance in your life. Embrace these exercises as tools of empowerment on your magickal journey towards financial success. Trust in the elemental foundations of financial magick and the transformative energies they bring to your financial reality.

Chapter 2 Conclusion:

In this chapter, we delved into the elemental foundations of financial magick, connecting with the energies of Earth, Air, Fire, Water, and Spirit. Each element brings unique attributes and wisdom that enrich our financial journey.

Earth taught us the importance of grounding our financial intentions, providing stability and a solid foundation for our prosperity. Air gifted us with intellectual clarity and wisdom, empowering us to make informed decisions in money matters. Fire ignited our passion and motivation, driving us towards financial success with unwavering determination.

Water reminded us of the significance of emotional intelligence, allowing us to navigate our financial experiences with balance and adaptability. Finally, Spirit connected us with universal abundance, reminding us that we are co-creators with the universe, deserving of prosperity.

As we continue our magickal journey towards financial abundance, let the elemental forces be our allies and guides. Embrace the grounding energy of Earth, the clarity of Air, the passion of Fire, the fluidity of Water, and the divine connection of Spirit.

In the subsequent chapters, we will delve deeper into the mysteries of financial magick, exploring astrological influences, elemental spells, crystal magick, and lunar cycles—all designed to enhance our financial manifestation and empower us as magickal beings.

Remember, you have the power to create a life of financial prosperity and fulfillment. Embrace the elemental foundations of financial magick and trust in the magickal forces that are always at your disposal. With the wisdom and energies of the elements by your side, the path to financial abundance unfolds before you. Embrace the magick and claim the financial prosperity that awaits you.

Chapter 3: Astrological Influences on Wealth Magick

Astrology plays a vital role in financial magick, and this chapter delves into the influence of various celestial bodies on wealth manifestation. You will understand how to tap into the power of the Sun for personal power, the Moon for intuition and emotional wealth, Mercury for communication and financial opportunities, Venus for financial harmony and attraction, Mars for assertive action, Jupiter for expanding abundance, and Saturn for building stability. The chapter also discusses aligning financial magick with the movements of the planets.

3.1: The Sun: Tapping into Personal Power and Success

In the realm of wealth magick, the celestial bodies hold significant influence over our financial journeys. The Sun, as the radiant center of our solar system, represents personal power, success, and the energy of manifestation. In this chapter, we explore the magickal significance of the Sun and how to harness its energy to tap into personal power and unlock the path to success in our financial endeavors.

1. The Sun's Magickal Energy

The Sun is the source of life and light, symbolizing vitality and the power of creation. In wealth magick, the Sun's energy serves as a catalyst for personal transformation and the manifestation of financial goals. Embracing the energy of the Sun empowers us to take bold actions and move confidently towards financial success.

2. Sun Invocation Ritual

Create a sacred space and set up an altar with representations of the Sun, such as a golden or yellow candle. Light the candle, and as the flame flickers, visualize the Sun's bright light filling the space with radiant energy. Stand in the warmth of the Sun's light, and repeat an invocation, such as:

"As the Sun rises in the sky, I invoke the power of personal power and success. May the light of the Sun infuse me with unwavering confidence and determination. I am a magnet for abundance, and success flows effortlessly towards me. With the Sun's blessings, I embrace my financial power and create the life of prosperity I desire."

3. Sun-Inspired Affirmations

Craft affirmations that align with the Sun's energy and repeat them daily. Affirmations such as "I am confident in my financial decisions," "I radiate success in all my endeavors," and "I am a powerful creator of abundance" help reprogram your subconscious mind, reinforcing a positive and successful mindset.

4. Solar Visualization Meditation

Sit or lie in a comfortable position and close your eyes. Take a few deep breaths, and imagine a bright and powerful Sun residing within your solar plexus, the area just above your navel. Visualize this inner Sun growing brighter and expanding, filling your entire body with its fiery light. Feel the warmth and energy infusing you with unwavering confidence and personal power. Bask in the glory of this internal Sun, knowing that you hold the power to manifest your financial desires.

5. Sun-Charged Prosperity Talisman

Create a prosperity talisman infused with the energy of the Sun. Choose a symbol or object that represents financial success to you, such as a gold coin or a sun-shaped pendant. Hold the talisman in your hands and visualize it being charged with the radiant energy of the Sun. Carry the talisman with you or place it in your wallet as a constant reminder of your financial power.

Conclusion:

The Sun, as a celestial force of personal power and success, holds a transformative influence over our financial magick practice. By tapping into the energy of the Sun, we unleash our innate potential to manifest abundance and prosperity.

As we continue our exploration of astrological influences on wealth magick, let the radiant energy of the Sun be a guiding light on our financial path. In the subsequent chapters, we will delve deeper into the magickal energies of the Moon, Mercury, Venus, Mars, Jupiter, Saturn, and the planetary dance, further enriching our financial magick practice.

Embrace the power of the Sun within you, unlocking personal power and success in your financial journey. Trust in the energy of the Sun to illuminate your path and lead you towards the manifestation of your financial goals. As you walk this magickal path, remember that you are a powerful co-creator, and with the Sun's blessings, the universe conspires to support your financial success.

3.2: The Moon: Harnessing Intuition and Emotional Wealth

In the realm of wealth magick, the Moon, with its ever-changing phases, holds profound influence over our emotions, intuition, and the ebb and flow of life. The Moon symbolizes the depths of our subconscious and our connection to the cycles of abundance. In this chapter, we explore the magickal significance of the Moon and how to harness its energy to tap into intuition and cultivate emotional wealth in our financial pursuits.

1. The Moon's Magickal Essence

The Moon's cycles influence the tides, emotions, and our connection to the unseen realms. In wealth magick, the Moon's energy guides us to embrace our intuition, navigate our emotions, and connect with the wealth of the soul. By aligning with the Moon's phases, we harmonize with the rhythm of abundance.

2. Moon Phases Meditation

Observe the different phases of the Moon—new, waxing, full, and waning—and their corresponding energies. Set aside time during each phase to meditate and attune yourself to the Moon's energy. During the new Moon, focus on new beginnings and intentions for financial growth. In the waxing Moon, amplify your financial goals and take inspired action. During the full Moon, express gratitude for the abundance in your life. In the waning Moon, release any limiting beliefs or emotions related to money.

3. Moonlit Intuition Ritual

On a clear night during the full Moon, go outside and bask in the Moon's radiant light. Close your eyes and feel the Moon's energy flowing through you. Invite the Moon to awaken your intuition and guide you on your financial path. Trust any intuitive insights or messages that come to you during this ritual. Carry a Moonstone or Labradorite crystal to enhance your intuition throughout the lunar cycle.

4. Moon Water Infusion

Harness the Moon's energy by creating Moon water—a magickal elixir infused with the Moon's essence. Place a glass container of purified water under the Moon's light overnight, allowing it to absorb the lunar energy. The next morning, drink the Moon water, imagining the Moon's energy flowing through you, awakening your intuition, and blessing your financial endeavors.

5. Lunar Gratitude Practice

Embrace a lunar gratitude practice during the full Moon phase. Take a moment to express gratitude for the financial abundance you have experienced and the opportunities that have come your way. Write a list of financial blessings and read it aloud under the full Moon. By cultivating a grateful heart, you open yourself to receiving more abundance from the universe.

Conclusion:

The Moon, with its mystical and cyclical nature, offers us a gateway to harnessing intuition and cultivating emotional wealth in our financial magick practice. By attuning ourselves to the Moon's phases, we align with the natural rhythms of abundance.

As we continue our exploration of astrological influences on wealth magick, let the Moon's energy be our guide in navigating the depths of our subconscious and connecting with the emotional aspects of our financial journey. In the subsequent chapters, we will delve deeper into the magickal energies of Mercury, Venus, Mars, Jupiter, Saturn, and the planetary dance, further enriching our financial magick practice.

Embrace the Moon's ever-changing light, harnessing intuition and emotional wealth in your financial pursuits. Trust in the Moon's guidance as you navigate the cycles of abundance and align with the wealth of your soul. As you walk this magickal path, know that you are in tune with the cosmic dance of abundance and prosperity.

3.3: Mercury: Communication and Financial Opportunities

In the realm of wealth magick, the planet Mercury governs communication, intellect, and the exchange of ideas. Mercury's influence opens the doors to financial opportunities through effective communication and strategic thinking. In this chapter, we explore the magickal significance of Mercury and how to harness its energy to enhance communication and attract favorable financial prospects.

1. Mercury's Magickal Energy

Mercury, as the messenger of the gods, represents the power of communication and the flow of information. In wealth magick, Mercury's energy empowers us to articulate our financial goals, network with like-minded individuals, and seize advantageous opportunities. Embracing Mercury's energy enhances our ability to manifest financial success through effective communication.

2. Mercury Invocation for Communication

Create a sacred space and invoke the energy of Mercury through a ritual. Light a yellow or orange candle, representing Mercury's vibrant energy, and say:

"Divine Mercury, the messenger of the gods, I call upon your energy of clear communication and strategic thinking. May your swift and agile nature guide my words and ideas in financial matters. With your blessing, I attract favorable opportunities and unlock the doors to prosperity. As above, so below."

3. Mercury's Winged Words

Enhance your communication skills by engaging in writing exercises. Write persuasive emails, proposals, or financial affirmations with intention and clarity. Visualize your words carrying the swift energy of Mercury, effortlessly reaching your intended audience and manifesting positive responses.

4. Networking with Mercury's Magick

Engage in networking events, workshops, or seminars related to finances and money matters. Approach these interactions with the energy of Mercury, being curious and open to exchanging ideas. Be an active listener and ask thoughtful questions. Networking with Mercury's energy will expand your circle of influence and attract new financial opportunities.

5. Financial Strategy Journal

Create a financial strategy journal to document your thoughts and ideas related to money. Use this journal to explore potential investment opportunities, savings plans, and other financial strategies. Write down any intuitive insights that come to you, trusting Mercury's guidance in strategic thinking.

6. Mercury Retrograde Preparations

During Mercury retrograde periods, which are known for communication challenges, take the opportunity to review and reassess your financial plans. Revisit your financial goals, check for any miscommunications or errors in financial documents, and use this time to refine your strategies. Approach Mercury retrograde with a mindset of adaptability and reflection.

Conclusion:

Mercury's influence on communication and financial opportunities empowers us to express our financial intentions clearly and strategically. By harnessing Mercury's energy, we attract favorable prospects and create a pathway to financial success.

As we continue our exploration of astrological influences on wealth magick, let Mercury be our ally in effective communication and strategic thinking. In the subsequent chapters, we will delve deeper into the magickal energies of Venus, Mars, Jupiter, Saturn, and the planetary dance, further enriching our financial magick practice.

Embrace Mercury's swift and agile energy, unlocking the potential of clear communication and favorable financial opportunities. Trust in the power of your words and ideas as you navigate the financial landscape with Mercury's guidance. As you walk this magickal path, remember that you possess the ability to manifest financial abundance through effective communication and strategic thinking.

3.4: Venus: Cultivating Financial Harmony and Attraction

In the realm of wealth magick, the planet Venus reigns as the embodiment of love, beauty, and attraction. Venus's energy goes beyond romantic love—it extends to the realm of finances, inviting us to cultivate harmony and attract abundance into our lives. In this chapter, we explore the magickal significance of Venus and how to harness its energy to foster financial harmony and magnetize prosperity.

1. Venus's Magickal Essence

Venus, the goddess of love and beauty, governs our sense of harmony and aesthetics. In wealth magick, Venus's energy guides us to create financial balance, cultivate self-worth, and attract abundance through an appreciation of beauty and value. Embracing Venus's energy enhances our ability to manifest financial prosperity with grace and allure.

2. Venusian Gratitude Ritual

Create a sacred space adorned with elements of beauty—flowers, crystals, and soothing music. Light a pink or green candle, representing Venus's loving and abundant energy. Close your eyes and take a few deep breaths. Express gratitude for the financial blessings in your life and the abundance yet to come. Embrace feelings of self-love and worthiness as you connect with the energy of Venus.

3. Beauty Magnetism Spell

Gather beautiful items that resonate with you—jewelry, gemstones, or art. Charge these items with Venusian energy by placing them on your altar or holding them in your hands. As you do this, visualize yourself becoming a magnet for financial abundance, attracting opportunities and resources effortlessly.

4. Financial Harmony Affirmations

Craft affirmations that embody Venus's energy of financial harmony and attraction. Repeat affirmations such as "I am a magnet for prosperity," "I attract abundance with ease and grace," and "My finances are in perfect harmony." Regularly affirming these statements will align your mindset with Venusian abundance.

5. Venusian Self-Care Practice

Engage in self-care practices that honor your self-worth and value. Pamper yourself with beauty rituals, such as taking relaxing baths or getting a massage. Treat yourself with kindness and compassion, recognizing that you deserve financial prosperity and abundance.

6. Cultivating Beauty in Finances

Create beauty in your financial space by organizing and decluttering. Arrange your financial documents and records in an aesthetically pleasing manner. Use beautiful stationery for financial planning or budgeting. Infusing beauty into your financial environment elevates its vibration and invites abundance to flow.

Conclusion:

Venus's influence on financial harmony and attraction invites us to cultivate self-love and embrace the beauty of abundance. By harnessing Venus's energy, we magnetize prosperity into our lives and create a sense of financial harmony and balance.

As we continue our exploration of astrological influences on wealth magick, let Venus be our guiding star in fostering financial beauty and attraction. In the subsequent chapters, we will delve deeper into the magickal energies of Mars, Jupiter, Saturn, and the planetary dance, further enriching our financial magick practice.

Embrace Venus's loving and abundant energy, cultivating financial harmony and attracting prosperity into your life. Trust in the beauty of your financial journey as you align with Venus's grace and allure. As you walk this magickal path, remember that you are a vessel of beauty and attraction, drawing financial abundance into your life with love and self-worth.

3.5: Mars: Taking Assertive Action for Financial Gains

In the realm of wealth magick, the planet Mars embodies the energy of action, assertiveness, and courage. Mars's influence empowers us to take bold steps towards our financial goals and seize opportunities with determination. In this chapter, we explore the magickal significance of Mars and how to harness its energy to take assertive action for financial gains.

1. Mars's Magickal Energy

Mars, the warrior planet, represents the drive and determination needed to achieve our desires. In wealth magick, Mars's energy propels us to move forward fearlessly, assert our financial intentions, and overcome obstacles that stand in the way of success. Embracing Mars's energy ignites our inner fire and motivates us to take action for financial gains.

2. Mars Empowerment Ritual

Create a sacred space and set up an altar with representations of Mars, such as a red candle or a symbol of a sword. Light the candle and visualize the flame representing the fire of Mars, igniting your inner courage and determination. Stand tall and repeat an empowerment affirmation, such as:

"I am a warrior of my financial destiny. With Mars's energy, I take assertive action to achieve my financial goals. I fearlessly pursue opportunities and overcome challenges with unwavering determination. As I align with Mars's fire, success and financial gains are mine to claim."

3. Financial Action Plan

Craft a clear and focused financial action plan. Break down your financial goals into actionable steps and set deadlines for each milestone. Embrace the energy of Mars as you take assertive action towards your goals, knowing that each step brings you closer to financial gains.

4. Courageous Decision-Making

Invoke the energy of Mars in moments of decision-making. When faced with financial choices, tap into your inner warrior and make courageous decisions. Trust your instincts and take calculated risks, knowing that Mars's energy supports your assertive action.

5. Mars-Charged Talisman

Create a Mars-charged talisman to carry with you as a symbol of your determination and assertiveness. Choose a red crystal or an object that resonates with Mars's energy. Hold the talisman in your hands and infuse it with your intentions for financial gains. Carry it with you as a reminder of your boldness and motivation.

6. Mars-Infused Daily Affirmations

Integrate Mars's energy into your daily routine with affirmations that reinforce your assertive action. Repeat affirmations such as "I am confident in taking bold steps towards financial gains," "I am a fearless warrior on my financial path," and "I embrace challenges and turn them into opportunities."

Conclusion:

Mars's influence on assertive action empowers us to fearlessly pursue our financial goals and claim abundant gains. By harnessing Mars's energy, we activate our inner warrior and courageously step into the realm of financial success.

As we continue our exploration of astrological influences on wealth magick, let Mars be our guiding force in taking assertive action for financial gains. In the subsequent chapters, we will delve deeper into the magickal energies of Jupiter, Saturn, and the planetary dance, further enriching our financial magick practice.

Embrace Mars's fire within you, taking assertive action for financial gains. Trust in your inner warrior as you fearlessly pursue opportunities and overcome obstacles on your financial journey. As you walk this magickal path, remember that you have the power to create financial success with boldness and determination.

3.6: Jupiter: Expanding Abundance and Opportunities

In the realm of wealth magick, the planet Jupiter is the epitome of expansion, growth, and abundance. Jupiter's energy invites us to embrace opportunities, broaden our horizons, and attract prosperity on a grand scale. In this chapter, we explore the magickal significance of Jupiter and how to harness its energy to expand abundance and attract favorable opportunities.

1. Jupiter's Magickal Essence

Jupiter, known as the "Great Benefic" in astrology, bestows blessings and favors upon those who align with its energy. In wealth magick, Jupiter's expansive influence opens doors to new possibilities and invites abundance to flow generously. Embracing Jupiter's energy empowers us to dream big, think optimistically, and attract boundless opportunities.

2. Jupiterian Abundance Altar

Create a dedicated Jupiterian abundance altar with symbols of expansion and prosperity. Use colors like royal blue and gold to represent Jupiter's majestic energy. Place a large citrine or other abundance crystals on the altar. Offer gratitude to Jupiter for the abundance in your life and invite its blessings for future growth.

3. Jupiter's Blessings Ritual

During a Jupiter-dominant day (Thursday) or Jupiter's planetary hour, perform a ritual to invoke Jupiter's blessings. Light a blue or gold candle, and express gratitude for the abundance you have experienced. Ask Jupiter to expand opportunities and bring new avenues of prosperity into your life. Open yourself to receive the blessings of Jupiter's abundance.

4. Abundance Visualization Meditation

Sit in a comfortable position, close your eyes, and take a few deep breaths. Visualize yourself surrounded by a brilliant, glowing light—the energy of

Jupiter's abundance. See this light expanding, encompassing all areas of your life. Embrace the feeling of boundless opportunities and prosperity entering your reality. Bask in the energy of Jupiter's generosity.

5. Jupiterian Affirmations for Abundance

Craft affirmations that resonate with Jupiter's energy of expansion and abundance. Repeat affirmations such as "I am open to receiving limitless abundance," "Opportunities for prosperity flow to me effortlessly," and "Jupiter's blessings enrich every area of my life." Regularly affirm these statements to align your mindset with the energy of Jupiter.

6. Jupiter Talisman for Prosperity

Create a Jupiter talisman to carry with you as a symbol of abundance and opportunity. Choose a symbol that represents Jupiter's energy, such as the planet's glyph or a symbolic image of expansion. Charge the talisman under the light of Jupiter or during a Jupiter-dominant day to amplify its energy.

Conclusion:

Jupiter's influence on expanding abundance and opportunities empowers us to dream big and attract boundless prosperity into our lives. By harnessing Jupiter's energy, we open ourselves to receive the generous blessings of growth and abundance.

As we continue our exploration of astrological influences on wealth magick, let Jupiter be our guiding star in expanding abundance and attracting favorable opportunities. In the subsequent chapters, we will delve deeper into the magickal energies of Saturn and the planetary dance, further enriching our financial magick practice.

Embrace Jupiter's boundless energy, expanding abundance, and opportunities in your financial journey. Trust in the benevolence of Jupiter as you welcome the blessings of prosperity and growth into your life. As you walk this magickal path, remember that you are a co-creator of abundance, and with Jupiter's guidance, the universe conspires to support your financial expansion.

3.7: Saturn: Building Long-Term Financial Stability

In the realm of wealth magick, the planet Saturn represents structure, discipline, and long-term planning. Saturn's energy teaches us the importance of laying a solid foundation for financial stability and enduring success. In this chapter, we explore the magickal significance of Saturn and how to harness its energy to build long-term financial stability.

1. Saturn's Magickal Essence

Saturn, often referred to as the "Great Teacher" in astrology, encourages us to embrace responsibility and discipline in our financial endeavors. In wealth magick, Saturn's influence fosters patience, perseverance, and the determination to overcome challenges. Embracing Saturn's energy empowers us to create a solid framework for long-term financial stability.

2. Saturnian Grounding Ritual

Create a sacred space and set up an altar with representations of Saturn, such as a black candle or a symbol of the planet's glyph. Light the candle and visualize its flame as a grounding force, anchoring you to the stability and structure of Saturn's energy. Stand tall and repeat a grounding affirmation, such as:

"With Saturn's energy as my guide, I embrace discipline and responsibility in my financial affairs. I lay a strong foundation for long-term stability and success. I am patient, persevering, and steadfast on my financial path. As I align with Saturn's wisdom, I build enduring prosperity."

3. Financial Planning with Saturn

Engage in thorough financial planning to align with Saturn's energy of structure and discipline. Create a budget that prioritizes saving and investments. Set realistic long-term financial goals and break them down into achievable milestones. Implement a systematic approach to managing your finances, ensuring stability and growth.

4. Saturnian Patience Meditation

Practice a meditation that cultivates patience and perseverance, traits aligned with Saturn's energy. Sit comfortably and focus on your breath. As you inhale and exhale, repeat the mantra "patience" or "perseverance" with each breath. Allow Saturn's patient energy to flow through you, knowing that long-term stability requires steady commitment.

5. Saturn's Blessings of Endurance

During a Saturn-dominant day (Saturday) or Saturn's planetary hour, perform a ritual to invoke Saturn's blessings. Light the black candle on your Saturn altar and express gratitude for the lessons and endurance Saturn brings to your financial journey. Ask for the strength to overcome challenges and build lasting stability.

6. Saturn Talisman for Financial Discipline

Create a Saturn talisman to carry with you as a reminder of financial discipline and responsibility. Choose a symbol that represents Saturn's energy, such as the planet's glyph or a symbol of endurance. Charge the talisman under the light of Saturn or during a Saturn-dominant day to enhance its energy.

Conclusion:

Saturn's influence on building long-term financial stability empowers us to embrace discipline and responsibility in our financial practices. By harnessing Saturn's energy, we lay the groundwork for enduring prosperity and success.

As we continue our exploration of astrological influences on wealth magick, let Saturn be our guiding teacher in building long-term financial stability. In the subsequent chapters, we will delve deeper into the magickal energies of the planetary dance, further enriching our financial magick practice.

Embrace Saturn's patient and disciplined energy, building long-term financial stability in your journey. Trust in the structure and endurance of Saturn as you create a solid foundation for enduring prosperity. As you walk this magickal path, remember that you hold the power to shape your financial destiny with responsibility and dedication.

3.8: The Planetary Dance: Aligning Your Financial Magick with the Stars

In the realm of wealth magick, the planets perform a celestial dance, each contributing its unique energy to our financial journey. By understanding and aligning with the planetary influences, we can enhance our financial magick and harness the full spectrum of cosmic energies. In this chapter, we explore the significance of the planetary dance and how to align our financial magick with the stars.

1. The Celestial Symphony

The planets in our solar system, each with its distinct attributes, form a celestial symphony that impacts our lives and financial experiences. Just as a conductor orchestrates an ensemble, we have the power to harmonize and direct these cosmic energies towards our financial goals.

2. Charting Your Financial Planets

Create your personal astrology chart to understand the positions of the planets at your birth. Identify the dominant planets in your chart that hold the most influence over your financial energies. For example, if Jupiter is prominent, you might focus on expansion and abundance, while Saturn's prominence could lead you to emphasize discipline and long-term planning.

3. Planetary Alignment Ritual

Design a planetary alignment ritual to align your financial magick with the stars. On a night when the dominant planet in your chart is visible, set up an altar with representations of the planets involved. Light a candle for each planetary energy, invoking its attributes and blessings. Meditate, visualizing the planets aligning harmoniously to empower your financial goals.

4. Planetary Hour Magick

Work with planetary hours to tap into the energies of the ruling planets during specific times of the day. Each planetary hour is governed by a different planet, offering a unique influence to your financial magick. Plan and perform financial rituals or spellwork during the corresponding planetary hours to enhance their potency.

5. Planetary Talismans and Sigils

Create planetary talismans or sigils to carry the energy of specific planets with you. Craft these symbols during auspicious planetary alignments or planetary hours. Empower them with your financial intentions and carry them as powerful reminders of your cosmic connection.

6. The Planetary Dance Meditation

Practice a meditation that connects you to the planetary dance. Close your eyes and visualize yourself as the conductor of this celestial symphony, directing the planets to align in perfect harmony for your financial goals. Feel the cosmic energies flowing through you, empowering your financial magick with celestial support.

Conclusion:

The planetary dance offers us a vast array of energies to empower our financial magick. By aligning with the stars and embracing the influence of each planet, we expand our potential for financial success and abundance.

3.9: The Celestial Symphony of Million-Dollar Magick

As we ascend through the celestial heights of astrological influences on wealth magick, a symphony of cosmic energies beckons us towards the realm of a million-dollar fortune. Each planetary dance orchestrates a unique melody of opportunities, aligning the universe in our favor as we embark on the magickal journey to financial abundance.

The Sun, with its radiant power, becomes the beacon that illuminates our path to personal power and success. As we bask in the warm glow of its energy, we tap into our inner strength and confidence, fortifying our resolve to manifest a million dollars with unwavering determination.

The Moon, the embodiment of intuition and emotional wealth, casts its ethereal light upon our financial decisions. Through lunar guidance, we attune ourselves to the ebbs and flows of the financial landscape, allowing our instincts to guide us towards lucrative opportunities and wise investments.

Mercury, the messenger planet, empowers our communication and opens doors to financial opportunities. With the magick of effective communication, we build bridges with potential partners, clients, and investors, expanding the reach of our financial ventures.

Venus, the planet of love and harmony, becomes the catalyst for cultivating financial abundance and attraction. As we infuse our financial endeavors with positivity and harmonious intent, we magnetize prosperity into our lives and create a harmonious flow of wealth.

Mars, the assertive warrior, inspires us to take bold and decisive action for financial gains. Embracing the magick of assertiveness, we fearlessly pursue our goals, overcoming obstacles with resilience and vigor.

Jupiter, the planet of expansion, blesses us with abundant opportunities and growth. By invoking the magick of expansion, we open ourselves to receive vast blessings and leverage opportunities that lead us closer to our million-dollar dreams.

Saturn, the planet of stability, guides us in building long-term financial security. Embracing the magick of discipline and perseverance, we lay the foundation for lasting wealth, ensuring our million-dollar fortune stands on solid ground.

As we align our financial magick with the celestial symphony of the planets, we enter into a cosmic dance of abundance. The Sun empowers our personal power, the Moon illuminates our intuition, Mercury opens doors, Venus harmonizes our endeavors, Mars drives our assertive action, Jupiter expands our opportunities, and Saturn bestows stability—all guided by the universal orchestration of the stars.

With each planetary influence harmoniously integrated, we find ourselves attuned to the cosmic rhythm, allowing the celestial energies to collaborate in manifesting our million-dollar aspirations. This divine symphony conducts us towards a prosperous future, where our financial dreams manifest with grace and precision.

As we continue our journey, let us remember that we are the co-creators of our financial destiny. We hold the baton to conduct this celestial symphony of million-dollar magick. With the wisdom of the planets as our guide and the universe as our witness, we embrace our divine role in shaping a prosperous reality that transcends the ordinary and embraces the extraordinary.

Amidst the cosmic dance of the celestial bodies, we unleash the magick within and around us, allowing the symphony of million-dollar magick to resonate through every fiber of our being. As we join the cosmic dance, we infuse our financial pursuits with celestial blessings, and the universe echoes its resounding support.

Embrace the celestial symphony of million-dollar magick and let the stars guide your financial aspirations towards fulfillment. The universe applauds your endeavor, for you are the magickal conductor of your own destiny, orchestrating a harmonious composition of prosperity and abundance in every note of your journey.

3.10: Practical Exercises for Chapter 3

3.1 The Sun: Tapping into Personal Power and Success

1. Solar Empowerment Visualization: Sit in a comfortable position and close your eyes. Visualize a radiant sun above you, emitting powerful rays of light. Envision these rays infusing you with confidence, self-assurance, and success. Feel the warmth of the sun's energy as it empowers you to take charge of your financial goals with unwavering determination.

2. Sun-Inspired Affirmations: Craft affirmations that resonate with the energy of the sun and personal power. Repeat affirmations such as "I am a powerful creator of my financial destiny," "I radiate confidence in my financial decisions," and "I embrace my innate ability to attract financial success." Regularly affirm these statements to strengthen your self-belief and financial empowerment.

3. Sun Ritual for Personal Success: On a sunny day, perform a ritual outdoors to connect with the energy of the sun. Face the sun and bask in its warmth, absorbing its energy into your being. Set clear intentions for personal and financial success, expressing gratitude for your achievements and envisioning future accomplishments.

3.2 The Moon: Harnessing Intuition and Emotional Wealth

1. Lunar Intuition Journal: Start a journal dedicated to recording your dreams, intuitive insights, and emotional experiences related to your financial journey. Pay close attention to the moon's phases and note any shifts in your emotions or intuitive hunches. Review your journal regularly to gain clarity and guidance in your financial decision-making.

2. Moonlit Release Ritual: During the waning moon phase, perform a release ritual to let go of any emotional blocks or limiting beliefs about money. Write down any financial fears or doubts on a piece of paper and then burn it under the moonlight. As the paper burns, visualize these obstacles transforming into empowering energy, clearing the path for financial abundance.

3. Moon Water Meditation: Create Moon water during the full moon by placing purified water in a glass container under the moonlight. The next morning, use this water in a meditation practice. As you drink the Moon water, envision the moon's energy activating your intuition and emotional wealth, guiding you on your financial path.

3.3 Mercury: Communication and Financial Opportunities

1. Mercury's Intellectual Boost: Engage in mind-stimulating activities related to finance, such as reading books on money management, attending financial workshops, or listening to podcasts about investments. Embrace Mercury's energy of communication and intellectual clarity to expand your financial knowledge and identify new opportunities.

2. Prosperous Communication Practice: Practice assertive and clear communication when discussing financial matters with others. Whether negotiating a salary, discussing investment opportunities, or communicating financial boundaries, channel Mercury's energy to express your needs and intentions confidently.

3. Mercury Retrograde Reflection: During Mercury retrograde periods, use this time for financial reflection and review. Revisit your financial plans, double-check important documents, and fine-tune your strategies. Be patient and avoid making major financial decisions during this period. Instead, focus on revising and reevaluating your plans.

3.4 Venus: Cultivating Financial Harmony and Attraction

1. Abundant Beauty Ritual: Create a sacred space adorned with beautiful items that resonate with Venus's energy—flowers, crystals, or artwork. Surround yourself with beauty and take a moment to appreciate the abundance in your life. Cultivate a sense of harmony and gratitude as you embrace Venus's energy of financial harmony and attraction.

2. Financial Attraction Crystal Grid: Design a crystal grid for financial attraction using abundance crystals like citrine, green aventurine, and pyrite. Place these crystals in a formation that resonates with you and your financial goals. As you activate the grid, visualize the energy of Venus drawing opportunities and prosperity towards you.

3. Venusian Gratitude Practice: During the full moon phase, perform a gratitude ritual dedicated to Venus. Write a heartfelt letter expressing your gratitude for the financial blessings in your life and the abundance you seek to attract. Read this letter aloud under the moonlight, trusting that Venus's energy will magnify your blessings.

3.5 Mars: Taking Assertive Action for Financial Gains

1. Mars Empowerment Affirmations: Craft affirmations that embody Mars's energy of assertive action and financial gains. Repeat affirmations such as "I am bold and fearless in pursuing my financial goals," "I take assertive action towards financial success," and "I embrace challenges and turn them into opportunities."

2. Mars-Charged Talisman: Create a Mars-charged talisman to carry with you as a symbol of your assertiveness and motivation. Choose a red crystal or an object that resonates with Mars's energy. Charge the talisman under the light of Mars or during a Mars-dominant day to amplify its energy.

3. Fearless Decision-Making Meditation: Practice a meditation that connects you with Mars's energy of fearlessness. Sit in a comfortable position and close your eyes. Visualize yourself embodying the assertiveness and confidence of Mars. Trust your instincts and envision yourself fearlessly making financial decisions that lead to success.

3.6 Jupiter: Expanding Abundance and Opportunities

1. Jupiterian Abundance Visualization: Sit in a comfortable position and close your eyes. Visualize yourself surrounded by a brilliant, glowing light—the energy of Jupiter's abundance. See this light expanding, encompassing all areas of your life. Embrace the feeling of boundless opportunities and prosperity entering your reality.

2. Jupiter's Blessings of Growth: During a Jupiter-dominant day (Thursday) or Jupiter's planetary hour, perform a ritual to invoke Jupiter's blessings. Light a blue or gold candle, and express gratitude for the abundance you have experienced. Ask Jupiter to expand opportunities and bring new avenues of prosperity into your life.

3. Jupiter Talisman for Prosperity: Create a Jupiter talisman to carry with you as a symbol of abundance and opportunity. Choose a symbol that represents Jupiter's energy, such as the planet's glyph or a symbol of expansion. Charge the talisman under the light of Jupiter or during a Jupiter-dominant day to enhance its energy.

3.7 Saturn: Building Long-Term Financial Stability

1. Saturnian Grounding Practice: Practice grounding exercises to align with Saturn's energy of discipline and responsibility. Spend time in nature, walk barefoot on the earth, or meditate while imagining roots growing from your body into the ground. Embrace the stability and structure of Saturn's energy in your financial planning.

2. Saturnian Financial Planning: Create a detailed and organized financial plan that reflects Saturn's energy of long-term stability. Set achievable financial goals with clear deadlines and steps to reach them. Embrace the discipline to stick to your plan, knowing that patience and perseverance lead to enduring success.

3. Saturn Talisman for Financial Discipline: Create a Saturn talisman to carry with you as a reminder of financial discipline and responsibility. Choose a symbol that represents Saturn's energy, such as the planet's glyph or a symbol of endurance. Charge the talisman under the light of Saturn or during a Saturn-dominant day to enhance its energy.

4. Saturn's Blessings Ritual: During a Saturn-dominant day (Saturday) or Saturn's planetary hour, perform a ritual to invoke Saturn's blessings. Light a black or dark blue candle to represent Saturn's energy. Express gratitude for the lessons and endurance Saturn brings to your financial journey. Ask for the strength to overcome challenges and build lasting stability.

3.8 The Planetary Dance: Aligning Your Financial Magick with the Stars

1. Celestial Alignment Meditation: Sit in a comfortable position and close your eyes. Visualize the planets in our solar system, each emitting its unique energy. Envision these energies aligning harmoniously with your financial goals. Embrace the cosmic support as you weave your financial magick with the celestial symphony.

2. Personal Astrology Chart Analysis: Consult an astrologer or use online resources to generate your personal astrology chart. Analyze the positions of the planets at your birth and identify the dominant planets that hold the most influence over your financial energies. Understand how these planetary energies impact your financial strengths and challenges.

3. Planetary Hour Magick: Work with planetary hours to tap into the energies of the ruling planets during specific times of the day. Each planetary hour is governed by a different planet, offering a unique influence to your financial magick. Plan and perform financial rituals or spellwork during the corresponding planetary hours to enhance their potency.

4. Planetary Talismans and Sigils: Create planetary talismans or sigils to carry the energy of specific planets with you. Craft these symbols during auspicious planetary alignments or planetary hours. Empower them with your financial intentions and carry them as powerful reminders of your cosmic connection.

5. The Planetary Dance Ritual: Design a ritual to honor the planetary dance and align your financial magick with the stars. Set up an altar with representations of the planets involved in your personal astrology chart. Light candles or incense for each planet and invoke their energies. Express gratitude for the celestial support in your financial endeavors.

6. Cosmic Synchronicity Journal: Start a journal dedicated to recording synchronicities and signs from the universe related to your financial goals. Pay attention to planetary alignments, moon phases, and any celestial events that coincide with significant financial developments. Reflect on how these cosmic occurrences influence your financial journey.

By embracing the astrological influences on wealth magick and aligning with the planetary energies, we deepen our connection to the cosmic forces that shape our financial reality. The exercises provided in this chapter offer practical ways to work with each planetary energy and integrate them into our financial magick practice.

As we continue our exploration of the mystical dance of the stars and its impact on our financial journey, remember that you are a co-creator with the universe. Embrace the celestial symphony and trust in the power of the stars as you weave your financial magick with cosmic grace. Let the wisdom of the planets guide your financial decisions, and may their energy support you on the path to abundance and prosperity. As you walk this magickal path, remember that you are a radiant participant in the planetary dance, and the universe conspires to support your financial manifestation and stability.

Chapter 3 Conclusion:

In Chapter 3, we delved into the captivating world of astrological influences on wealth magick, exploring the profound impact of celestial energies on our financial journey. Each planet in our solar system contributes its unique attributes, guiding us towards abundance, success, and stability. By understanding and harnessing the energies of the planets, we unlock the power to manifest our financial desires and shape our financial destiny.

The Sun empowers us to tap into our personal power and embrace success with unwavering confidence. The Moon illuminates our intuition and emotional wealth, offering guidance through the ebb and flow of financial decisions. Mercury enhances our communication and opens doors to new financial opportunities.

Venus showers us with the blessings of financial harmony and attraction, drawing abundance towards us. Mars ignites our assertive action and propels us towards financial gains. Jupiter expands our abundance, bringing new opportunities and prosperity.

Saturn, the Great Teacher, teaches us discipline and responsibility, laying the foundation for long-term financial stability. The planetary dance orchestrates a celestial symphony, harmonizing the energies of the cosmos to empower our financial magick.

Through practical exercises, rituals, and meditations, we have embraced the wisdom of each planetary energy, aligning our financial intentions with the stars. By co-creating with the universe and understanding our unique astrological influences, we journey towards enduring prosperity and success.

As we conclude our exploration of astrological influences on wealth magick, let us remember that the celestial forces are ever-present, guiding and supporting our financial path. Embrace the cosmic connection and trust in the magick of the stars as you manifest abundance and financial well-being. Walk confidently in the planetary dance, knowing that you hold the keys to unlocking the cosmic riches that await you. As you embark on this magickal journey, may the stars light your way, and may your financial dreams become a luminous reality.

Chapter 4: Elemental Spells for Financial Prosperity

Building on the knowledge of elemental associations from Chapter 2, this chapter presents practical spells that utilize Earth, Air, Fire, Water, and Spirit to materialize financial goals. You will learn how to use these elemental energies to boost mental clarity, ignite ambition, and find emotional balance in financial matters. The chapter also guides you in crafting comprehensive wealth spells that integrate all the elemental forces.

4.1: Earth Spells: Materializing Financial Goals

In this chapter, we delve into the realm of Earth spells, where the energy of grounding and manifestation reigns supreme. The element of Earth provides us with stability, abundance, and the power to materialize our financial goals. Through these spells, we tap into the fertile soil of prosperity and sow the seeds of abundance in our lives.

1. Earth Abundance Altar: Create an Earth abundance altar in your sacred space or a corner of your home. Place symbols of prosperity, such as coins, gemstones like citrine and green aventurine, and plants representing growth and abundance. As you spend time near the altar, visualize your financial goals coming to fruition and aligning with the energy of the Earth.

2. Manifestation Jar Spell: Take a glass jar and fill it with small crystals, coins, and herbs associated with prosperity. Write your financial intentions on a piece of paper and place it inside the jar. Seal the jar with a green or gold ribbon, symbolizing abundance and wealth. Every day, hold the jar in your hands, infusing it with your intent, and visualize your financial goals manifesting. Keep the jar in a prominent place as a powerful reminder of your intentions.

3. Earthly Gratitude Ritual: Perform a gratitude ritual dedicated to the Earth element and its role in providing us with abundance. Go outdoors and find a quiet spot in nature. Take off your shoes and connect with the Earth beneath your feet. Express gratitude for the financial blessings you have received and those that are on their way. Embrace the Earth's nurturing energy, knowing that it supports your financial growth.

4. Prosperity Pentacle Spell: Draw or print a pentacle symbol on a piece of paper. In each point of the pentacle, write down a specific financial goal you wish to achieve. Place the paper on a flat surface and surround it with green candles. Light the candles, one by one, while focusing on each financial goal. As the candles burn, visualize the pentacle radiating with the energy of prosperity, empowering your financial endeavors.

5. Earth Abundance Charm: Create an Earth abundance charm to carry with you as a symbol of prosperity. Choose a small, green drawstring bag or pouch. Fill it with a combination of prosperity symbols, such as a lodestone, a small citrine crystal, and a few coins. As you add each item, imbue it with your financial intentions. Carry the charm with you daily to attract abundance and opportunities.

6. Green Candle Money Spell: On a Thursday (associated with the planet Jupiter and financial growth), take a green candle and carve your financial goal into it with a pin or toothpick. Anoint the candle with a few drops of essential oil, such as cinnamon or bergamot, representing abundance. Light the candle and visualize the flame amplifying your financial desires. Let the candle burn completely as a symbol of the continuous flow of financial prosperity.

7. Earth Element Abundance Meditation: Sit comfortably in a quiet space and close your eyes. Take deep breaths and visualize yourself surrounded by lush greenery and fertile soil. Feel the Earth's energy grounding and stabilizing y

ou. Envision your financial goals as seeds planted in the Earth, absorbing the energy of growth and abundance. As you meditate, feel the seeds sprouting and your financial desires becoming a reality.

Conclusion:

The Earth spells presented in this chapter offer potent tools for materializing financial goals and embracing the stable abundance of the Earth element. As you work with the energy of Earth, remember that you hold the power to sow the seeds of prosperity in your life. Trust in the magick of the Earth and your ability to manifest financial abundance as you embark on this elemental journey. May the fertile energy of the Earth support you in achieving your financial dreams and cultivating lasting prosperity.

4.2: Air Spells: Boosting Mental Clarity and Financial Decision-Making

In this chapter, we explore the realm of Air spells, where the energy of intellect and communication empowers us to enhance our mental clarity and make informed financial decisions. The element of Air invites us to embrace the power of knowledge and wisdom as we navigate the financial landscape with confidence and precision.

1. Clarity Visualization Spell: Sit in a quiet and comfortable space. Close your eyes and take deep breaths, allowing your mind to clear. Visualize a gentle breeze of Air surrounding you, sweeping away any mental fog or confusion related to your finances. See yourself filled with mental clarity, making decisions with ease and precision. Embrace the empowering energy of Air as it enhances your financial perception.

2. Financial Decision Incense Ritual: Choose an incense blend or single herb associated with mental clarity, such as lavender or rosemary. Light the incense and allow the fragrant smoke to fill your space. As you inhale the aroma, focus on the financial decision you need to make. Invite the guidance of Air to bring clarity and wisdom to your mind, helping you see the best path forward.

3. Elemental Mind Mapping: Create a mind map to explore different financial possibilities and opportunities. Use colors and symbols to represent various financial goals and decisions. As you build the mind map, let the energy of Air inspire you with new ideas and insights. This exercise will help you organize your thoughts and gain a comprehensive view of your financial options.

4. Financial Journaling Practice: Start a journal dedicated to your financial journey and decision-making process. Write down your thoughts, emotions, and observations related to money matters. Use this journal to reflect on your financial goals, challenges, and the steps you are taking to achieve them. The act of journaling will help you gain mental clarity and identify areas that need attention.

5. Communication with the Financial Air Spirits: Create an altar with representations of the Air element, such as feathers, incense, and a clear crystal. Sit in front of the altar and light a yellow candle, symbolizing mental clarity. Invite the spirits of the Air element to guide your financial decisions and communicate any insights or messages they may have. Trust in their guidance as you move forward in your financial endeavors.

6. Prosperity Affirmations with Air Visualization: Craft affirmations that enhance your mental clarity and financial decision-making. Repeat affirmations such as "I am clear and focused in my financial choices," "I make wise decisions that lead to abundance," and "I embrace the guidance of the Air element in my financial journey." As you recite these affirmations, visualize a gentle breeze of Air carrying your intentions and filling your mind with clarity and confidence.

7. Air Element Mindfulness Meditation: Sit comfortably in a quiet space and focus on your breath. With each inhale, imagine yourself drawing in the fresh and invigorating Air energy. With each exhale, release any mental clutter or doubts. Embrace the present moment and the clarity that Air brings to your mind. Feel the Air element cleansing your thoughts and empowering you to make sound financial decisions.

Conclusion:

Air spells provide us with the tools to harness the power of mental clarity and wise decision-making in our financial endeavors. As you embrace the energy of Air, you strengthen your ability to analyze situations, weigh options, and make informed choices that align with your financial goals. May the power of Air guide you towards prosperity and financial wisdom as you navigate the currents of the financial world. Trust in the clarity that Air brings and use it as a beacon to illuminate your path to lasting financial abundance.

4.3: Fire Spells: Igniting Passion and Ambition for Wealth

In this chapter, we immerse ourselves in the realm of Fire spells, where the energy of passion and ambition ignites the flames of wealth manifestation. The element of Fire empowers us to embrace our inner drive and take assertive action towards our financial goals with unwavering enthusiasm.

1. Prosperity Candle Spell: Select a red or gold candle to represent the Fire element and financial passion. Carve symbols of abundance, such as dollar signs or runes for wealth, onto the candle. Anoint the candle with a few drops of essential oil, like cinnamon or ginger, to infuse it with the energy of passion and ambition. Light the candle, focusing on your financial aspirations and the determination to achieve them. Let the flame burn as a symbol of the fiery passion that fuels your wealth journey.

2. Fiery Visualization Meditation: Sit in a comfortable space and close your eyes. Visualize a blazing fire within your solar plexus, the seat of your personal power. Feel the warmth of the flames spreading throughout your body, igniting your passion for financial success. Embrace the intensity of Fire as it fuels your ambition and drives you towards the fulfillment of your financial dreams.

3. Prosperity Dance Ritual: Engage in a dynamic dance ritual to connect with the Fire element's passionate energy. Play uplifting and rhythmic music that resonates with your financial aspirations. Move your body freely, allowing the Fire within to express itself through movement. As you dance, affirm your financial goals with each step, infusing them with fiery energy.

4. Ambitious Goal-Setting Spell: Write down your most ambitious financial goals on a piece of paper. Place the paper on a fire-safe dish or cauldron. Light the edges of the paper on fire, watching it burn with the intensity of your ambition. As the flames consume the paper, visualize your goals being ignited into reality. Embrace the fiery energy of transformation as you take assertive action towards your aspirations.

5. Passionate Financial Affirmations: Craft affirmations that embody the energy of Fire and financial ambition. Repeat affirmations such as "I am driven to achieve my financial goals," "My passion for success fuels my actions," and "I am a fearless and ambitious creator of wealth." Recite these affirmations daily to stoke the flames of determination within you.

6. Fiery Prosperity Talisman: Create a talisman that represents your financial ambition and passion. Choose a symbol that resonates with Fire, such as a phoenix or a fire symbol. Charge the talisman under the light of a candle or during a Mars-dominant day to enhance its fiery energy. Carry the talisman with you as a reminder of your relentless pursuit of wealth.

7. Fire Element Empowerment Ritual: Perform a ritual to connect with the Fire element and receive its empowering energy. Light a bonfire or a candle outdoors and meditate beside it. Invite the energy of Fire into your being, feeling its transformative power. Express gratitude for the passion and ambition it bestows upon you in your financial journey.

Conclusion:

Fire spells ignite the flames of passion and ambition within us, driving us towards our financial goals with unwavering enthusiasm. As we embrace the fiery energy, we find the determination and courage to take bold action and make our dreams of wealth a reality. Trust in the passion that Fire ignites within you and let it blaze a trail of prosperity on your financial path. May the power of Fire propel you towards abundance and financial success as you harness its fiery energy in your wealth magick.

4.4: Water Spells: Embracing Emotional Balance for Financial Success

In this chapter, we immerse ourselves in the realm of Water spells, where the energy of emotions and intuition guides us towards emotional balance for financial success. The element of Water empowers us to embrace our feelings, release any emotional blockages, and flow with the currents of abundance.

1. Abundance Bath Ritual: Draw a warm bath and add a few drops of essential oils associated with prosperity, such as ylang-ylang or bergamot. As you soak in the water, envision any emotional stress or financial worries dissolving and being washed away. Embrace the healing and cleansing properties of Water, allowing it to restore emotional balance and invite financial abundance into your life.

2. Financial Moon Journal: Create a special journal dedicated to recording your emotions and financial experiences during different moon phases. Pay attention to how your emotions affect your financial decisions and how the moon's cycles influence your feelings. Reflect on these insights to find emotional balance and align your financial actions with the lunar rhythms.

3. Release and Flow Visualization: Sit in a quiet space and close your eyes. Visualize a gentle river flowing in front of you, symbolizing the flow of abundance. See any emotional blockages or negative beliefs about money floating away on the river's current. Release any attachments to past financial experiences that no longer serve you. Embrace the emotional freedom that comes with the flow of Water, allowing you to attract financial success.

4. Prosperity Moon Water Elixir: On a clear night, place a container of purified water under the light of the full moon. Let the water absorb the moon's energy overnight. The next morning, take a sip of the moon-charged water and affirm your financial intentions. As you drink, feel the emotional balance and intuition of Water empowering your financial decisions.

5. Intuitive Abundance Tarot Spread: Use a tarot deck to perform a special intuitive abundance spread. Select cards that represent your current emotional state, financial challenges, and opportunities for growth. Allow your intuition to guide you as you interpret the messages from the cards. Use this spread as a tool to gain emotional clarity and navigate your financial path with wisdom.

6. Emotionally Balanced Spending Practice: Practice mindful spending by evaluating your emotional state before making financial decisions. Ask yourself if you are making purchases based on emotional impulses or genuine needs. Pause and assess whether the expense aligns with your financial goals and values. Embrace emotional balance to make conscious financial choices.

7. Water Element Altar: Create a Water element altar with representations of Water, such as seashells, a small bowl of water, and blue candles. Sit in front of the altar and meditate, inviting the energy of Water to flow within you. Express gratitude for the emotional guidance it provides and for the ability to achieve financial success with emotional balance.

Conclusion:

Water spells invite us to embrace emotional balance and intuition as we navigate our financial journey. By acknowledging and releasing emotional blockages, we allow the flow of abundance to enter our lives. As we harness the power of Water, we gain the wisdom to make conscious financial decisions and to trust our intuition in matters of wealth.

May the energy of Water wash away any emotional barriers and guide you towards emotional harmony in your financial pursuits. Trust in the intuitive guidance of Water as you flow with the currents of abundance, and may your emotional balance lead you to lasting financial success. As you embrace the element of Water in your wealth magick, may you find inner peace and prosperity on your financial path.

4.5: Spirit Spells: Invoking Universal Guidance in Money Matters

In this chapter, we delve into the realm of Spirit spells, where the energy of the divine and universal guidance empowers us to seek wisdom and direction in our money matters. The connection to Spirit allows us to align our financial decisions with higher purpose and invite divine support into our wealth journey.

1. Divine Guidance Meditation: Sit in a peaceful space and close your eyes. Take deep breaths, allowing yourself to relax and center. Visualize a bright, divine light shining from above, representing universal guidance. Feel this light enveloping you with love and wisdom. Ask for divine guidance in your financial endeavors, trusting that the answers will come when you need them.

2. Spiritual Gratitude Ritual: Create a ritual to express gratitude to the divine for the financial blessings you have received and those that are on their way. Light a white or gold candle to symbolize divine energy. Offer words of thanks for the guidance and support you receive in your money matters. Trust that the universe is conspiring in your favor as you walk your financial path.

3. Intentional Affirmations for Spiritual Alignment: Craft affirmations that invoke spiritual alignment in your financial journey. Repeat affirmations such as "I am guided and supported by the divine in all my financial decisions," "My financial actions are aligned with my higher purpose," and "I attract financial opportunities that serve my soul's growth." Embrace these affirmations as mantras to invite divine assistance into your money matters.

4. Angelic Prosperity Invocation: Call upon your guardian angels and spirit guides to support you in your financial goals. Light a white candle and write a letter to your angels, expressing your financial intentions and desires. Speak from the heart, inviting their guidance and assistance. Trust that your angelic allies are listening and will provide you with signs and guidance along the way.

5. Universal Abundance Sigil: Design a sigil that represents universal abundance and divine guidance. Combine symbols that resonate with spiritual energy and prosperity. Meditate on the sigil, infusing it with your financial intentions and aligning it with higher purpose. Keep the sigil in a sacred space or carry it with you as a powerful symbol of divine support.

6. Financial Tarot Reading with Spirit Connection: Perform a tarot reading with the intention of connecting with Spirit for financial insights. Take a few moments to center yourself and call upon your spirit guides or higher self for guidance. Shuffle the cards with your question in mind, and lay them out. Interpret the reading with openness to the spiritual messages that come through.

7. Divine Gratitude Journaling: Start a gratitude journal dedicated to your spiritual connection and financial growth. Each day, write down the spiritual insights and guidance you receive regarding your money matters. Reflect on how the divine presence influences your financial decisions and trust that you are always guided on the right path.

Conclusion:

Spirit spells offer us the profound opportunity to invoke universal guidance and align our financial decisions with higher purpose. By connecting to the divine and expressing gratitude for the spiritual support we receive, we invite abundance and prosperity into our lives. Trust in the wisdom of the universe and the guidance of the divine as you navigate your financial journey.

May the energy of Spirit inspire you to walk a path of soulful prosperity and may your financial decisions be guided by divine wisdom. As you embrace the spiritual connection in your wealth magick, may you find solace in knowing that you are always supported and guided on your financial path. Embrace the presence of Spirit in your money matters, and may it lead you to abundance and fulfillment beyond your wildest dreams.

4.6: The Magickal Elements United: Crafting Comprehensive Wealth Spells

In this chapter, we explore the art of uniting the magickal elements - Earth, Air, Fire, Water, and Spirit - to create comprehensive wealth spells that harness the full spectrum of energies available to us. By combining the power of these elements, we elevate our financial magick to new heights, bringing forth abundance, prosperity, and alignment with our highest purpose.

1. Elemental Prosperity Altar: Create a comprehensive prosperity altar that represents all five elements. Incorporate items that correspond to each element, such as crystals for Earth, incense for Air, candles for Fire, a bowl of water for Water, and symbols of spirit, such as feathers or angel figurines. Use this altar as a focal point for your wealth spells, invoking the energies of all the elements to amplify your intentions.

2. Elemental Wealth Jar Spell: Take a glass jar and add representative items for each element: a small crystal for Earth, a feather or incense for Air, a red or gold ribbon for Fire, a few drops of essential oil for Water, and a white feather or angelic symbol for Spirit. Write your financial intentions on a piece of paper and place it in the jar. Seal the jar and shake it gently to blend the elemental energies together. Keep the jar on your prosperity altar as a potent wealth spell.

3. Elemental Abundance Ritual Bath: Prepare a ritual bath infused with the energies of all the elements. Add a handful of sea salt for Earth, a few drops of essential oil for Air, a red or orange candle for Fire, and a few drops of floral essence for Water. Light the candle and immerse yourself in the bath, visualizing the elemental energies enveloping you in abundance. Embrace the harmony of the elements and envision your financial desires manifesting effortlessly.

4. Elemental Prosperity Meditation: Sit in a quiet space and imagine the five elements surrounding you in a circle. Begin by grounding yourself with the Earth's energy, then breathe in the clarity of Air, the passion of Fire, the emotional balance of Water, and the guidance of Spirit. As you embrace each element, feel their collective power infusing your financial intentions with divine energy.

5. Elemental Wealth Sigil: Design a sigil that combines symbols representing all five elements to embody the essence of comprehensive wealth. Meditate on the sigil, charging it with your financial desires and the unity of the elements. Carry the sigil with you or place it on your prosperity altar as a magickal charm that harmonizes the elemental forces in your favor.

6. Sacred Elemental Circle for Wealth: Create a sacred circle, calling upon the energies of each element to bless your wealth magick. Stand at each quarter of the circle and invoke the qualities of Earth, Air, Fire, Water, and Spirit. As you move around the circle, feel the energies merging and aligning to support your financial goals. Conclude the ritual by standing at the center, embracing the united power of the elements within you.

7. Elemental Wealth Manifestation Spell: Craft a comprehensive wealth spell that includes rituals, visualizations, and affirmations to invoke the energies of all five elements. Perform the spell during a significant astrological event, such as a new moon or a planetary alignment, to amplify its potency. Trust in the collective energy of the elements to manifest your financial desires with divine synchronicity.

Conclusion:

Crafting comprehensive wealth spells that unite the magickal elements is a potent way to elevate your financial magick and align it with the full spectrum of energies available to you. As you combine the power of Earth, Air, Fire, Water, and Spirit, you create a harmonious symphony of abundance and prosperity in your life.

May the unity of the elements empower your financial intentions and lead you to lasting wealth and fulfillment. Embrace the magickal dance of the elements as you co-create with the universe to manifest your financial dreams. As you explore the art of comprehensive wealth spells, may the magickal forces of the elements unite to support and bless your financial journey in miraculous ways.

4.7: The Magickal Circle of Financial Prosperity

In this chapter, we delve into the concept of the Magickal Circle—a sacred space where we gather and harness the collective energy of the elements for financial prosperity. The Magickal Circle serves as a powerful tool to amplify our intentions and create a harmonious flow of abundance in our lives.

1. Setting the Circle of Intentions: Begin by cleansing the space where you will create the Magickal Circle. Use sage, incense, or a purification ritual to clear any negative energies. Stand in the center of the space and take deep breaths, grounding yourself to the Earth. Visualize a sphere of golden light surrounding you, forming the boundary of the Magickal Circle.

2. Invoking the Elements: Starting at the North, call upon each element one by one, moving in a clockwise direction. As you face each direction, invite the energies of Earth, Air, Fire, Water, and Spirit into the circle. Feel the power of each element intensifying as it joins the circle, and acknowledge their support in your financial endeavors.

3. The Prosperity Altar: Set up a prosperity altar at the center of the Magickal Circle. Place items representing abundance, such as coins, green candles, crystals, and symbols of wealth, on the altar. Add representations of the elements to acknowledge their presence within the circle. This altar becomes a focal point to channel your financial intentions.

4. Chanting and Affirmations: Stand at the center of the circle and raise your energy through chanting or reciting affirmations related to financial prosperity. Use phrases like "Abundance flows to me from all directions," "I am aligned with the universe's wealth," and "I am open to receive the blessings of financial success." Allow the vibrations of your voice to resonate throughout the Magickal Circle.

5. Elemental Visualization: With the elements present in the circle, visualize each element's energy manifesting around you. See the stability of Earth beneath your feet, the clarity of Air expanding your vision, the passion of

Fire igniting your ambition, the emotional balance of Water nurturing your intentions, and the guidance of Spirit directing your path to prosperity.

6. Energy Charging Ritual: Hold your hands palms down over the prosperity altar, infusing it with your financial intentions. Imagine a vibrant, golden light radiating from your hands, charging the altar with your desired financial outcomes. Feel the energy of the Magickal Circle amplifying your intentions, as the elements collaborate to bring your desires to fruition.

7. Gratitude and Closing: Express gratitude to the elements for their presence and support in the Magickal Circle. Slowly move in a counterclockwise direction, thanking each element as you bid them farewell. As you return to the North, imagine the golden sphere of the circle dissipating, but know that the energies of the elements remain within you, continuing to work in harmony for your financial prosperity.

Conclusion:

The Magickal Circle of Financial Prosperity is a potent space to unite with the energies of the elements and invoke their support for abundance and wealth. As you harness the collective power of Earth, Air, Fire, Water, and Spirit, you open yourself to infinite possibilities in your financial journey.

May the Magickal Circle serve as a sacred container to amplify your financial intentions and align you with the flow of prosperity. Embrace the power of the elements as they collaborate in perfect harmony, guiding you towards lasting financial success. As you work within the Magickal Circle, trust in the universe's support and know that the energies of abundance are always available to you.

4.8: Maintaining the Magickal Momentum

In this chapter, we explore the essential practices and techniques to maintain the magickal momentum of our financial prosperity journey. Just as a flowing river requires continuous nourishment, so does our financial magick demand ongoing attention and dedication to sustain its potency.

1. Regular Prosperity Affirmations: Incorporate daily prosperity affirmations into your routine to reinforce your positive mindset about finances. Repeating affirmations such as "I attract abundance effortlessly," "Money flows to me in unexpected ways," and "I am worthy of financial success" keeps your focus on the positive aspects of wealth creation.

2. Element-Specific Check-Ins: Set aside time to connect with each elemental energy individually. Reflect on the stability of Earth, the clarity of Air, the passion of Fire, the emotional balance of Water, and the guidance of Spirit. Ensure that you are nurturing and balancing each element within you to maintain the harmony of your financial magick.

3. Regular Spell Reinforcement: Revisit the spells and rituals from earlier chapters periodically. Whether it's the Elemental Wealth Jar, the Prosperity Candle Spell, or the Magickal Circle of Financial Prosperity, reinforcing these magickal practices keeps the energies alive and active, continuously empowering your financial intentions.

4. Gratitude and Abundance Journaling: Maintain a gratitude and abundance journal to record your daily experiences of financial blessings and synchronicities. Expressing gratitude for even the smallest signs of prosperity keeps you aligned with abundance and attracts more positive outcomes into your life.

5. Mindful Spending and Budgeting: Stay conscious of your spending habits and budgeting practices. Regularly review your financial goals and adjust your budget as needed to ensure you are aligning your financial decisions with your aspirations.

6. Visualization and Meditation: Continue to practice visualization and meditation to keep your financial intentions at the forefront of your mind. Engaging in regular meditative sessions allows you to maintain a clear focus on your goals and strengthens your connection to the universe's flow of abundance.

7. Collaboration and Community: Engage with like-minded individuals who share your financial aspirations. Collaborating with a community focused on prosperity and abundance provides support, encouragement, and inspiration to maintain your magickal momentum.

8. Adaptation and Flexibility: Stay open to adapting your financial plans and strategies as circumstances change. Embrace the flexibility to shift course when needed, knowing that the universe always has alternative paths to manifest your desires.

Conclusion:

Maintaining the magickal momentum of your financial prosperity journey requires dedication, consistency, and an unwavering belief in the power of your intentions. By reinforcing the spells, rituals, and practices from this guide, you strengthen your connection to the elemental energies and the universe's abundance.

May the magickal momentum of your financial prosperity journey carry you towards enduring wealth and fulfillment. As you continue to work with the elements, trust that the universe is always conspiring in your favor. Embrace the ongoing process of manifesting financial abundance and know that you hold the power to create the life of prosperity and success you desire.

4.9: Uniting the Magickal Elements for Million-Dollar Prosperity

In the magickal tapestry of financial prosperity, the elements weave a harmonious dance, uniting their energies to support the manifestation of a million-dollar fortune. As we explore the elemental spells for financial prosperity, we discover the power of their convergence and how they can be harnessed to create a magickal symphony that leads us to our desired destination.

Earth spells materialize our financial goals, grounding our intentions with practicality and providing a stable foundation for million-dollar ambitions. By utilizing the magick of earth, we anchor our dreams in reality, transforming them into tangible manifestations that take shape in the material realm.

Air spells boost our mental clarity and financial decision-making, becoming the guiding winds that steer us towards lucrative opportunities. Embracing the magick of air, we gain the wisdom and intellectual acuity to make informed choices that lead us closer to our million-dollar dreams.

Fire spells ignite the flames of passion and ambition, fueling our pursuit of wealth and success. Like a blazing fire, the magick of fire infuses us with the drive and determination to take bold action, overcoming obstacles and forging ahead on the path to financial abundance.

Water spells embrace emotional balance, allowing us to navigate the ever-changing tides of the financial landscape. By harmonizing our emotions, we maintain clarity and resilience, ensuring that nothing stands in the way of our million-dollar aspirations.

Spirit spells invoke universal guidance, connecting us to the infinite flow of abundance. As we align with the magick of spirit, we attune ourselves to the cosmic currents that lead us towards prosperity, knowing that we are supported and guided on our magickal journey.

But the true magick of making a million dollars lies in the alchemical fusion of these elemental energies. Like a skilled alchemist, we blend the elements into a comprehensive wealth spell, creating a potent brew that amplifies the potency of our financial manifestations.

Within this magickal amalgamation, we activate the synergy of the elements, each element enhancing the power of the others. Earth provides a solid foundation, air lends clarity to our intentions, fire ignites our passion, water maintains emotional balance, and spirit connects us to universal abundance. In this sacred union, the elemental forces converge, and the magickal momentum intensifies towards the million-dollar mark.

As we wield this magickal alchemy, we must remember that the journey to a million dollars with magick requires dedication, perseverance, and alignment with ethical principles. We are the architects of our own destiny, and the magick of making a million dollars is not simply about material gain but about personal growth, transformation, and creating a positive impact in the world.

With each element harmoniously integrated, we become the master conductors of our financial destiny, orchestrating the symphony of million-dollar prosperity. With the universe as our witness and the elements as our allies, we step boldly into the realm of abundance, embracing the magick that lies within and around us.

So let the elements unite, and let the magick unfold. The universe awaits your command, and the million-dollar fortune beckons. As we journey together on this magickal path, may the elemental forces guide us towards a prosperous future filled with abundance and blessings untold.

4.10: Practical Exercises for Chapter 4

4.1 Earth Spells: Materializing Financial Goals

1. Prosperity Crystal Grid: Create a crystal grid using wealth-attracting crystals such as citrine, pyrite, and green aventurine. Place the crystals in a geometric pattern on a clean surface. In the center, add a paper with your million-dollar financial goal written on it. Focus your intention on the grid, visualizing the crystals amplifying your wealth manifestation. Leave the grid in place, regularly charging it with your intentions.

4.2 Air Spells: Boosting Mental Clarity and Financial Decision-Making

1. Mind Mapping Your Financial Strategy: Use the element of Air to enhance your mental clarity and decision-making. Create a mind map or flowchart of your million-dollar strategy. Include various financial avenues, investment options, and potential business ventures. Use different colored pens to represent each aspect. As you expand the map, you'll gain insights into the most viable paths to achieving your financial goal.

4.3 Fire Spells: Igniting Passion and Ambition for Wealth

1. Envisioning Financial Success Ritual: Light a red or gold candle to represent the element of Fire and the energy of passion and ambition. Sit in front of the candle, focusing on its flame, and visualize your life with a million dollars. Feel the excitement and determination to accomplish your financial dreams. As the candle burns, know that the energy of Fire is igniting your passion and propelling you towards the wealth you desire.

4.4 Water Spells: Embracing Emotional Balance for Financial Success

1. Emotional Release and Visualization: Fill a bowl with water and add a few drops of calming essential oil like lavender or chamomile. Sit comfortably and place your hands on the water's surface. Allow any emotional blockages related to money or abundance to surface. Release these emotions into the water, feeling them wash away. Visualize yourself immersed in a calm and abundant ocean of emotions, knowing that emotional balance supports your journey to making a million dollars.

4.5 Spirit Spells: Invoking Universal Guidance in Money Matters

1. Celestial Guidance Meditation: Find a quiet space to meditate. Light a white candle to represent the element of Spirit. Close your eyes and envision yourself surrounded by a celestial glow, connecting you to the wisdom of the universe. Seek guidance from the higher realms on your million-dollar quest. Trust in the messages or intuitive insights you receive, knowing that the universe is supporting and guiding you on your path to financial abundance.

4.6 The Magickal Elements United: Crafting Comprehensive Wealth Spells

1. Million-Dollar Abundance Spell: Integrate all four elements—Earth, Air, Fire, and Water—in a comprehensive wealth spell. Utilize a green candle to represent financial abundance. Surround it with wealth-attracting crystals, herbs, and symbols of prosperity. Light the candle and focus your intention on making a million dollars. Channel the energy of the elements and the universe to manifest your financial aspirations. As the candle burns, release the spell's energy to the universe with gratitude.

4.7 The Magickal Circle of Financial Prosperity

1. Circle Casting for Financial Success: Before engaging in any financial endeavors, cast a magickal circle for financial success. Stand at the center and visualize a protective circle of light forming around you. Call upon the elements and any deities or spirits associated with wealth to bless your endeavors. Set your intention for success and financial abundance within the circle. Work within this magickal space, knowing that it will amplify your efforts to make a million dollars.

4.8 Maintaining the Magickal Momentum

1. Daily Affirmations and Gratitude Practice: Combine daily affirmations with a gratitude journal to maintain the momentum of your magickal practice. Each morning, recite affirmations related to making a million dollars. Throughout the day, express gratitude for the blessings and opportunities that come your way. This practice keeps you aligned with the magickal energies and fosters a positive mindset for financial success.

By incorporating these practical exercises into your magickal practice, you harness the power of the elements to manifest your million-dollar reality. Embrace the magickal potential within you, and let the energies of Earth, Air, Fire, Water, and Spirit guide you on your path to financial abundance. Trust in the universe's support, and know that you have the magickal tools to make your financial dreams come true.

Chapter 4 Conclusion:

In this chapter, we explored the transformative power of elemental spells for financial prosperity. By harnessing the energies of Earth, Air, Fire, Water, and Spirit, we unlocked the key to manifesting abundance, aligning our intentions with the universe's flow of prosperity.

From grounding our financial goals with Earth spells to boosting mental clarity with Air spells, igniting passion and ambition through Fire spells, embracing emotional balance with Water spells, and invoking universal guidance through Spirit spells, we delved into the depth of each element's influence on our wealth journey.

Crafting comprehensive wealth spells that united the magickal elements in harmony, we created a sacred space within the Magickal Circle to amplify our intentions and embrace divine support. We learned to maintain the magickal momentum by affirming our prosperity, checking in with each element, reinforcing our spells, and cultivating gratitude.

Throughout this chapter, we embraced the art of financial magick as a journey of self-discovery, empowerment, and co-creation with the universe. By combining the wisdom of the elements and our conscious intentions, we unlocked the doors to lasting financial success.

As we continue on our financial prosperity path, let us remember that the power to manifest abundance lies within us. Embrace the elemental energies and trust in the universe's support to guide you towards your desired financial goals. Remember that prosperity is not just about monetary gains, but also about finding fulfillment, purpose, and joy in your financial journey.

May the wisdom of the elements and the magickal momentum of your financial prosperity spells lead you to a life of abundance, well-being, and profound spiritual growth. Embrace the power within you, and may your wealth magick journey be one of magic, transformation, and unlimited potential.

Chapter 5: Crystal Magick for Prosperity

Crystals are potent tools in magick, and this chapter focuses on their use for financial prosperity. You will learn how to select and cleanse prosperity crystals, charge them with wealth energies, and create crystal grids to attract abundance. The chapter also introduces crystal elixirs and carrying crystal allies for daily prosperity, as well as using crystals for creating an abundant living environment.

5.1: The Power of Crystals in Financial Magick

In this chapter, we explore the enchanting realm of crystal magick and its potent influence on financial prosperity. Crystals, with their unique energetic vibrations, have been revered for centuries as powerful tools for manifestation, healing, and spiritual growth. Discover how to harness the inherent energies of crystals to attract wealth, abundance, and success into your life.

1. Crystal Consciousness and Prosperity: Understanding the consciousness of crystals is fundamental to their effective use in financial magick. Each crystal carries a distinct energy that resonates with specific aspects of wealth, such as abundance, manifestation, opportunity, and intuition. Learn to attune to the energetic frequencies of crystals to amplify your intentions for financial prosperity.

2. Selecting Prosperity Crystals: Explore a diverse range of crystals renowned for their association with prosperity. Green Aventurine attracts luck and wealth, Citrine stimulates abundance and manifestation, Pyrite fosters financial success, and Clear Quartz amplifies intentions. Select crystals that align with your financial goals and intuition, forming a unique and personal collection to support your wealth journey.

3. Cleansing and Charging Prosperity Crystals: Before using crystals for financial magick, cleanse their energies to remove any prior imprints and charge them with your intentions. Use methods such as smudging, moonlight cleansing, or placing them in a bowl of saltwater to purify their energies. Charge the crystals with your financial desires through meditation, visualization, or placing them under a candle's light.

4. Creating a Crystal Grid for Prosperity: Design a crystal grid to intensify the energies of your prosperity intentions. Arrange your selected crystals in a geometric pattern, such as a flower of life or a crystal grid template. Place a clear quartz crystal at the center to amplify the grid's power. As you activate the grid, focus your intentions on financial abundance, allowing the crystals to work synergistically.

5. Crystal Elixirs for Wealth Energies: Infuse water with the energies of prosperity crystals by creating crystal elixirs. Immerse cleaned crystals in a glass jar of purified water and leave them to charge in the sunlight or moonlight. The charged water becomes a potent elixir that you can consume daily, infusing your being with the vibrational frequencies of abundance.

6. Carrying Crystal Allies for Daily Prosperity: Select a prosperity crystal to carry with you throughout the day. Keep it in your pocket, purse, or wear it as jewelry to maintain a continuous connection with its energies. Allow the crystal to be a constant reminder of your financial intentions, empowering you to make inspired decisions and attract prosperity in every endeavor.

7. Wealthy Home: Crystal Decor for Abundant Living: Transform your living space into a sanctuary of abundance by incorporating prosperity crystals into your home decor. Place crystals strategically, such as Citrine in the wealth corner (southeast), Pyrite near the entrance for financial opportunities, and Green Aventurine in your workspace to enhance prosperity and productivity.

Conclusion:

Crystals hold an ancient and potent wisdom that can be harnessed to enhance financial prosperity. As you delve into the world of crystal magick, remember to respect and honor these beautiful gifts of the Earth. Embrace the power of crystals to align your energy with abundance and attract financial success into your life.

May the magic of crystals amplify your financial intentions and bring forth the wealth and prosperity you seek. As you integrate crystals into your financial magick, may you discover a profound connection with the Earth's energy, empowering you to manifest your desires and create a life of abundance and fulfillment. Let the enchantment of crystals guide you on your journey to prosperity and open the door to endless possibilities for financial success.

5.2: Selecting and Cleansing Prosperity Crystals

In this section, we delve deeper into the art of selecting and cleansing prosperity crystals. Choosing the right crystals for your financial magick and ensuring their purity and potency are crucial steps in harnessing their energies for abundance and prosperity.

1. Crystal Consciousness: Understanding Vibrational Resonance Each crystal possesses a unique vibrational frequency that resonates with specific energies. When selecting prosperity crystals, consider their metaphysical properties and the qualities they embody, such as abundance, wealth, manifestation, and success. Allow your intuition to guide you, as certain crystals may speak to you more strongly than others.

2. Researching Prosperity Crystals Explore various crystals associated with financial abundance and prosperity. Research their properties, historical significance, and traditional uses in wealth magick. Some well-known prosperity crystals include Citrine, Green Aventurine, Pyrite, Jade, and Clear Quartz. Familiarize yourself with their attributes to make informed choices for your collection.

3. Trusting Your Intuition When selecting prosperity crystals, trust your intuition and let your heart guide you. Hold each crystal in your hand, close your eyes, and tune into its energy. Pay attention to any sensations, visions, or emotions that arise. A crystal that feels warm, tingly, or resonates with positive energy is likely a good match for your financial intentions.

4. Cleansing Your Prosperity Crystals Before using your selected prosperity crystals for financial magick, it is essential to cleanse them of any prior energies they may carry. Crystals can absorb and store energies from their surroundings, so purifying them ensures their optimal performance.

Smudging: Pass the crystals through the smoke of white sage, palo santo, or other cleansing herbs to clear their energies.

Sunlight and Moonlight: Leave the crystals in direct sunlight or under the light of the full moon for a few hours or overnight to cleanse them.

Saltwater Bath: Submerge the crystals in a bowl of purified water mixed with a bit of sea salt. Rinse them thoroughly afterward.

5. Intention Setting After cleansing, hold each prosperity crystal in your hands and set your financial intentions clearly and purposefully. Visualize the crystals being charged with the energy of abundance, attracting wealth and prosperity into your life. Feel a connection between your intentions and the crystal's energies as you infuse them with your desires.

6. Storing and Caring for Your Prosperity Crystals To maintain the potency of your prosperity crystals, store them in a safe and sacred space. Consider using a wooden box, velvet pouch, or a dedicated altar. Avoid placing them in cluttered or chaotic areas to preserve their harmonious energies. Regularly cleanse and charge them to keep their vibrations pure and powerful.

Conclusion:

Selecting and cleansing prosperity crystals is an essential aspect of crystal magick for financial abundance. By understanding the vibrational resonance of each crystal and trusting your intuition, you can create a powerful collection of crystals aligned with your financial intentions. Remember to cleanse and charge your crystals regularly to maintain their effectiveness in attracting wealth and prosperity into your life.

May the process of selecting and cleansing prosperity crystals deepen your connection with the energies of abundance and open pathways to financial success. As you work with these magical gifts from the Earth, may their transformative energies guide you towards a life of prosperity, fulfillment, and limitless possibilities. Embrace the enchantment of crystals in your financial magick, and may they serve as steadfast allies on your journey to prosperity and abundance.

5.3: Charging Crystals for Wealth Attraction

In this section, we explore the art of charging crystals for wealth attraction. Charging is a sacred process that infuses crystals with your financial intentions, amplifying their energy and aligning them with the vibration of abundance. By charging your prosperity crystals, you create potent tools for manifesting financial success.

1. Set the Intentions: Before charging your prosperity crystals, take a moment to set clear and focused intentions for your financial goals. Reflect on what you desire to attract—whether it's increased wealth, new opportunities, career success, or financial security. Visualize these intentions as if they have already come to fruition, feeling the joy and abundance associated with achieving your financial dreams.

2. Choose an Amplifying Method: There are several methods to charge your prosperity crystals, each bringing its unique energy and potency to the process. Choose the method that resonates with you and aligns with your intentions:

a. Sunlight Charging: Place your crystals in direct sunlight for a few hours, preferably during the morning or afternoon when the sun's energy is most vibrant. Visualize the sunlight infusing your crystals with the energy of growth, vitality, and prosperity.

b. Moonlight Charging: Charge your crystals under the light of the full moon or during the waxing moon phase. The moon's energy is gentle and nurturing, facilitating emotional balance and intuition, essential qualities for financial success.

c. Candle Flame Charging: Hold your crystals above the flame of a green or gold candle. As you do so, envision the flame igniting the energy of abundance within the crystals, fueling your financial intentions.

d. Earth Charging: Bury your prosperity crystals in the soil of a potted plant or directly in the earth for 24 hours or longer. This method connects your crystals with the grounding energies of Mother Earth, symbolizing the materialization of your financial desires.

3. Invocation and Affirmations: During the charging process, speak aloud or silently recite affirmations that resonate with your financial intentions. State your affirmations confidently and with conviction, infusing them with emotion and belief. For example:

"I am a magnet for wealth and abundance."

"Money flows to me effortlessly and abundantly."

"I attract lucrative opportunities in every area of my life."

"I am open and receptive to financial blessings from the universe."

4. Gratitude and Connection: Express gratitude to the universe, the elements, and the crystals for their support in manifesting your financial intentions. Feel a deep connection with the energy of the crystals, recognizing that they are now charged and aligned with your desires.

5. Cleansing after Charging: Once your crystals are charged with your financial intentions, it is essential to cleanse them before use. This step ensures that any residual energies from the charging process are removed, leaving the crystals pure and ready to work with your financial magick.

Conclusion:

Charging crystals for wealth attraction is a sacred and transformative practice. By infusing your prosperity crystals with clear intentions, utilizing various charging methods, and expressing gratitude, you create powerful tools that align with the energy of abundance.

May the process of charging your prosperity crystals deepen your connection with the universe's flow of prosperity. As you work with these charged crystals, may they serve as catalysts for financial success, opening doors to opportunities, and guiding you towards the fulfillment of your financial dreams. Embrace the power of charged crystals in your financial magick, and may they continue to radiate abundance and attract prosperity into every aspect of your life.

5.4: Crystal Grids for Financial Abundance

In this section, we delve into the fascinating world of crystal grids for financial abundance. Crystal grids are sacred geometric arrangements of prosperity crystals that work synergistically to amplify intentions and manifest your financial desires. Creating a crystal grid empowers you to tap into the harmonious energy of crystals and attract wealth and prosperity with focused intent.

1. Set Your Intentions: Before assembling your crystal grid, clarify your financial intentions. What specific goals do you wish to achieve? Whether it's increasing income, finding a new job, launching a successful business, or achieving financial stability, clearly define your desires to align the grid's energy with your intentions.

2. Selecting Prosperity Crystals: Choose a variety of prosperity crystals that resonate with your financial goals. Combine crystals known for attracting wealth, success, opportunity, and motivation. Citrine, Pyrite, Green Aventurine, Tiger's Eye, and Clear Quartz are excellent choices. Consider incorporating a clear quartz point to amplify the grid's energy.

3. Sacred Space Preparation: Find a quiet and peaceful space to create your crystal grid. Cleanse the area with sage, incense, or a purification ritual to ensure a harmonious and energetically clear environment. Take a few moments to ground yourself and set your mind and heart on your financial intentions.

4. Crystal Grid Layout: Select a sacred geometric pattern that resonates with you, such as a flower of life, seed of life, or a personal symbol that represents abundance. Lay out the pattern on a flat surface, such as a wooden board or a cloth, and place a clear quartz point at the center as the central amplifier.

5. Activating the Grid: Starting from the center, place each prosperity crystal on the corresponding points of the sacred geometric pattern. As you place each crystal, state your financial intentions clearly and vividly. Visualize the energy of abundance flowing from the central clear quartz point, spreading through the entire grid, and radiating out into the universe.

6. Connecting with the Grid: Once all the crystals are in place, use a clear quartz wand or your finger to energetically connect the crystals. Trace the lines of the sacred geometric pattern, envisioning a web of energy linking each crystal, creating a powerful network of prosperity.

7. Empowering Your Grid: To further empower your crystal grid, perform a short meditation or visualization. Imagine yourself already in possession of the financial abundance you desire. Feel the joy, excitement, and gratitude associated with your financial success. Send this powerful energy into the crystal grid, reinforcing your intentions.

8. Gratitude and Maintenance: Express gratitude to the crystals, the grid, and the universe for their support in manifesting your financial desires. Leave the crystal grid in place for as long as you feel necessary, continuing to charge it with your intentions and positive energy regularly. You can also reactivate the grid whenever you feel the need to strengthen your financial magick.

Conclusion:

Crystal grids for financial abundance are potent tools that combine the energies of prosperity crystals to amplify your financial intentions. As you harness the power of sacred geometry and the harmonic resonance of crystals, you tap into the infinite potential of the universe to manifest your financial dreams.

May the creation of your crystal grid be a profound and transformative experience, aligning you with the energies of abundance and prosperity. Embrace the magic of crystal grids, and may their radiant energy attract wealth, success, and fulfillment into every aspect of your financial journey. Trust in the power of your intentions and the assistance of the crystals as you walk the path of financial abundance with confidence and grace.

5.5: Crystal Elixirs: Infusing Water with Wealth Energies

In this section, we explore the enchanting practice of creating crystal elixirs to infuse water with wealth energies. Crystal elixirs, also known as gemstone waters, harness the vibrational properties of prosperity crystals to enhance your well-being and attract financial abundance into your life. This sacred and potent elixir empowers you to align your body, mind, and spirit with the frequency of wealth.

1. Choosing the Right Crystals: Select prosperity crystals that are safe for creating crystal elixirs. Non-toxic crystals such as Clear Quartz, Citrine, Green Aventurine, and Amethyst are ideal choices. Ensure the crystals are cleansed and charged before creating the elixir to optimize their energetic effects.

2. Preparing the Water: Use purified or spring water to create your crystal elixir. Choose a glass jar or bottle that can hold the desired amount of water. To amplify the elixir's energy, consider using a clear quartz crystal to place in the water, in addition to the prosperity crystals.

3. Charging the Water: Before submerging the prosperity crystals in the water, set your intentions for the elixir. Focus on the financial intentions you wish to infuse into the water. Hold the jar in your hands, close your eyes, and visualize the water becoming charged with the energies of abundance and prosperity.

4. Infusing the Water: Place the cleansed prosperity crystals in the jar of water, making sure they are fully submerged. Optionally, add the clear quartz crystal to amplify the elixir's energy. Seal the jar and allow the crystals to infuse the water for a minimum of 4-6 hours or overnight. The longer the infusion time, the stronger the elixir's potency.

5. Charging under Moonlight or Sunlight: To further charge the crystal elixir, leave the jar under the light of the full moon or in direct sunlight. The moon's energy enhances intuition and emotional balance, while the sun energizes and empowers the elixir with vitality and strength. Retrieve the jar before sunrise or sunset to prevent the water from becoming energetically drained.

6. Harvesting the Elixir: Once the infusion is complete, carefully remove the prosperity crystals from the jar, and your crystal elixir is ready for use. You can choose to keep the elixir at room temperature or refrigerate it for a refreshing and charged drink.

7. Drinking the Crystal Elixir: Sip the crystal elixir mindfully, allowing its energies to nourish your body, mind, and spirit. As you drink, focus on your financial intentions and visualize abundance flowing into your life. Feel the crystal elixir working in harmony with your being, aligning you with the frequency of wealth.

8. Elixir Maintenance: Recharge your crystal elixir regularly by placing it in sunlight or moonlight. Replace the prosperity crystals in the elixir every few weeks to ensure the elixir's energy remains vibrant and potent.

Conclusion:

Crystal elixirs are a sacred and delightful way to infuse water with wealth energies, providing a harmonious connection to the vibrational frequencies of prosperity crystals. As you sip the crystal elixir, may you feel the flow of abundance and financial well-being entering every aspect of your life.

May the crystal elixir serve as a catalyst for aligning your energy with wealth and prosperity. Embrace the enchantment of this magickal elixir, and may it open the gates to financial success, nourishing your soul and guiding you towards a life of abundance, fulfillment, and unlimited possibilities. Trust in the power of the crystal elixir and the prosperity crystals as you continue your journey towards financial prosperity with confidence and grace.

5.6: Carrying Crystal Allies for Daily Prosperity

In this section, we explore the practice of carrying crystal allies for daily prosperity. By keeping prosperity crystals close to you throughout the day, you establish a constant connection with their energies, empowering you to attract wealth and abundance into every aspect of your life.

1. Selecting Your Crystal Allies: Choose one or more prosperity crystals that resonate with your financial intentions. Consider crystals such as Citrine for wealth and success, Pyrite for financial abundance, Green Aventurine for luck and opportunity, or Tiger's Eye for motivation and determination. Trust your intuition and select crystals that feel aligned with your goals.

2. Programming Your Crystals: Before carrying your crystal allies, program them with your specific financial intentions. Hold each crystal in your hands and focus on your desired outcomes. State your intentions clearly and firmly, visualizing your financial goals coming to fruition. As you do so, imagine the crystals absorbing and amplifying these intentions.

3. Creating a Pouch or Charm: To carry your crystal allies conveniently, create a small pouch or charm to keep them together. You can use a small fabric pouch, a small drawstring bag, or a piece of cloth tied with a ribbon. You may also consider using a locket or a small glass vial to hold the crystals.

4. Charging Your Pouch or Charm: Place your programmed prosperity crystals in the pouch or charm and hold it between your hands. Close your eyes and visualize the pouch being filled with a radiant golden light, representing the energy of abundance and prosperity. Feel the crystals vibrating with this powerful energy.

5. Carrying Your Crystal Allies: Keep your pouch or charm containing the crystal allies with you throughout the day. You can carry it in your pocket, purse, or hang it as a pendant around your neck. Whenever you touch or see the pouch, take a moment to reinforce your financial intentions and connect with the crystals' energies.

6. Regular Cleansing and Recharging: To maintain the effectiveness of your crystal allies, cleanse and recharge them regularly. Cleanse the crystals using your preferred method, such as smudging or placing them under running water. Recharge them by exposing them to sunlight or moonlight, allowing them to soak up the energies of the celestial bodies.

7. Trusting the Synchronicity: As you carry your crystal allies, trust in the synchronicities and opportunities that come your way. Be open to receiving the abundance the universe has in store for you. Stay aligned with your financial intentions and take inspired action towards your goals.

Conclusion:

Carrying crystal allies for daily prosperity is a powerful and tangible way to stay connected with the energies of abundance and wealth. As you keep your programmed crystals close to you, you create a constant reminder of your financial intentions and align your energy with prosperity.

May the practice of carrying crystal allies empower you to attract financial success, opportunities, and abundance into your life. Embrace the magic of these crystal allies, and may they serve as steadfast companions on your journey to financial prosperity. Trust in their vibrational frequencies and the guidance of the universe as you manifest your dreams with grace and determination.

5.7: Wealthy Home: Crystal Decor for Abundant Living

In this section, we explore the art of using crystal decor to create a wealthy home that radiates the energies of abundance, prosperity, and well-being. By strategically placing prosperity crystals throughout your living space, you can amplify the vibrations of wealth and attract positive energies into your home.

1. Identify Key Areas: Take a moment to identify key areas in your home that are associated with financial prosperity and abundance. These areas include:

The Wealth Corner: In Feng Shui, the southeast corner of your home is considered the wealth corner. Place prosperity crystals, such as Citrine or Pyrite, in this area to enhance its energies.

The Workspace: If you have a home office or workspace, adorn it with crystals like Green Aventurine or Clear Quartz to boost productivity, attract success, and invite financial opportunities.

The Entrance: Create a positive first impression by placing prosperity crystals near the entrance of your home. This can include a small bowl of tumbled stones or a crystal geode.

The Living Room: Infuse the heart of your home with prosperity by placing a crystal grid or a collection of prosperity crystals in the living room.

2. Choose the Right Crystals: Select prosperity crystals that harmonize with each area's purpose. Citrine is widely known for its ability to attract wealth and success. Green Aventurine invites luck and prosperity. Pyrite symbolizes abundance and financial prosperity. Amethyst fosters intuition and wise financial decision-making. Clear Quartz amplifies the energies of all crystals, making it a versatile addition to any space.

3. Create a Crystal Grid: Craft a crystal grid for your home using prosperity crystals. Choose a sacred geometric pattern that resonates with your intentions. Place the grid in the wealth corner or any area that symbolizes financial abundance for you. Activate the grid with your intentions, and visualize your home being filled with the energies of prosperity.

4. Abundance Altar: Designate a special area in your home as an abundance altar. Arrange prosperity crystals, candles, and any objects that symbolize wealth and prosperity on this altar. Use the altar for meditation, affirmations, or any rituals related to attracting financial abundance.

5. Feng Shui Enhancements: Incorporate Feng Shui principles into your crystal decor to maximize the flow of prosperity. Ensure that the energy in your home flows freely by decluttering and organizing your space. Keep pathways clear and place prosperity crystals strategically to invite positive energy.

6. Cleansing and Charging: Regularly cleanse and charge your prosperity crystals to maintain their vibrant energy. Smudge the crystals with sage or use other preferred cleansing methods. Charge them by placing them in sunlight or moonlight, allowing them to absorb the energies of the celestial bodies.

7. Intentional Display: As you place prosperity crystals around your home, do so with intention. With each crystal's placement, visualize the energies of abundance and prosperity infusing the space. State your financial intentions clearly and feel the energy of the crystals resonating with your desires.

Conclusion:

Creating a wealthy home with crystal decor is a sacred and powerful practice. By mindfully placing prosperity crystals throughout your living space, you invite the energies of abundance, prosperity, and positive vibrations into your life.

May the crystal decor in your home be a reflection of your financial intentions, attracting wealth, success, and well-being into every aspect of your life. Embrace the magic of crystal decor, and may your home become a sanctuary of abundance, where prosperity flows freely and opportunities abound. Trust in the power of your intentions and the energies of the crystals as you transform your living space into a haven of abundant living.

5.8: Crystal Allies for Million-Dollar Magick

In the realm of prosperity magick, crystals stand as powerful allies, infused with ancient energies that resonate with our deepest desires for financial abundance. As we explore the magick of crystals for prosperity, we unveil the secrets of selecting, charging, and utilizing these sacred gemstones to manifest a million-dollar fortune.

The power of crystals in financial magick lies in their unique vibrations, each carrying a distinct energy that aligns with specific intentions. By carefully selecting crystals that resonate with wealth and abundance, we harness their energies to amplify our million-dollar manifestations.

Cleansing the prosperity crystals becomes the sacred ritual that purifies their energy, ensuring they are free from any past influences that may hinder their magickal potency. By imbuing them with our pure intent, we prepare them as powerful vessels for attracting wealth and prosperity.

Charging the crystals with wealth energies infuses them with our million-dollar intentions. Like a magickal battery, we connect with the crystals, transferring our desires into them and creating a direct channel for the universe to respond to our financial aspirations.

Creating crystal grids becomes the magickal blueprint for financial abundance. By arranging prosperity crystals in sacred geometric patterns, we amplify their energies, forming a magickal network that radiates our intentions far and wide, drawing prosperity from all directions.

Crystal elixirs become the enchanted elixirs that infuse water with wealth energies, allowing us to consume the essence of prosperity on a cellular level. By ingesting the magickal elixirs, we align our vibration with abundance and open ourselves to receiving the universe's bountiful blessings.

Carrying crystal allies becomes the daily practice that keeps us attuned to the frequency of prosperity. By keeping prosperity crystals close, we are constantly reminded of our million-dollar dreams, enhancing our focus and determination as we walk the path to financial abundance.

Wealthy home becomes the sacred sanctuary adorned with crystal decor, aligning the energy of our living space with prosperity. By infusing our home with the vibrations of abundance, we create a magickal atmosphere that supports our financial manifestations and fosters a prosperous mindset.

As we embrace the magick of crystals for million-dollar prosperity, we step into a realm where the energies of the earth converge with our desires, forming a potent magickal union. These sacred gemstones become our companions on the journey to financial abundance, anchoring our intentions and aligning us with the cosmic flow of prosperity.

As we carry our crystal allies and immerse ourselves in the vibrations of their energies, we become a magnet for financial blessings and opportunities. Each crystal becomes a guiding light that leads us towards the manifestation of a million-dollar fortune.

But amidst this magickal journey, we must remain mindful that the true power of crystals lies in our belief and intention. They serve as catalysts for our inner magick, empowering us to unleash the potential that resides within. With the sacred wisdom of the crystals as our guide, we merge our earthly aspirations with the celestial energies, opening the floodgates to financial abundance.

In this magickal dance with crystals, we become the architects of our financial destiny. Through the sacred synergy of the crystal allies, we attune ourselves to the universal symphony of prosperity, aligning our energies with the million-dollar vibration that awaits us.

Let the crystals be our steadfast companions as we venture boldly towards financial abundance. With the brilliance of their energies and the power of our intentions, we embrace the magick of making a million dollars and awaken the universe to respond in kind.

As we continue this enchanting journey with our crystal allies, may the celestial forces conspire to weave the tapestry of prosperity that leads us to a million-dollar destiny. The universe stands ready to shower us with blessings, and the crystals stand as living proof of the magick that lies within and around us.

Embrace the crystal allies, and let the magick unfold. The path to a million dollars awaits, and with each step we take, the crystals resonate, amplifying the vibrations of our desires and calling forth the abundance that is rightfully ours.

5.9: Practical Exercises for Chapter 5

Exercise 1: Million-Dollar Money Visualization with Crystals

Visualization is a powerful technique to align your mind and energy with your financial goals. Combine it with the energy of prosperity crystals to supercharge your manifestation process.

Materials:

A quiet and peaceful space

A green or gold cloth (optional, for added symbolism)

A selection of prosperity crystals (e.g., citrine, green aventurine, pyrite)

Comfortable seating or cushions

Instructions:

1. Find a serene space where you can sit comfortably without distractions.

2. Lay the green or gold cloth on the ground or a flat surface, signifying prosperity and abundance.

3. Hold the prosperity crystals in your hands and take a few deep breaths to center yourself.

4. Close your eyes and envision a clear mental image of yourself holding a check or a bank statement with a million-dollar balance.

5. Feel the joy, excitement, and gratitude as if you've already achieved your financial goal. Imagine how your life has changed for the better.

6. As you continue the visualization, allow the energy of the prosperity crystals to flow into the mental image, amplifying the vibration of abundance and prosperity.

7. Stay in this visualization for at least 5-10 minutes, immersing yourself completely in the experience.

8. Open your eyes and place the crystals on the green or gold cloth, allowing them to absorb the energy of the visualization.

9. Whenever you feel doubtful or uncertain about your financial journey, return to this visualization to reinforce your million-dollar intention.

Exercise 2: Crystal-Infused Money Magnet Talisman

Create a crystal-infused money magnet talisman to carry with you and attract financial opportunities wherever you go.

Materials:

A green or gold drawstring pouch

A selection of prosperity crystals (e.g., citrine, pyrite, green aventurine)

A piece of green or gold paper

A pen with green or gold ink

Instructions:

1. Find a quiet space where you can focus your energy on creating the talisman.

2. Hold the green or gold drawstring pouch in your hands and set the intention that it will become a powerful money magnet.

3. Take the piece of green or gold paper and write your million-dollar affirmation or intention on it using the green or gold ink.

4. Place the paper inside the pouch, symbolizing the containment of your financial desires.

5. Add the prosperity crystals to the pouch, charging them with the energy of your million-dollar goal.

6. Close the pouch with the drawstring, sealing the energy within.

7. Hold the talisman in your hands and infuse it with your intention, visualizing it attracting financial opportunities and prosperity.

8. Carry the talisman with you wherever you go, whether in your pocket, purse, or on a necklace.

9. Whenever you encounter financial decisions or opportunities, hold the talisman in your hand, and reaffirm your million-dollar intention.

Exercise 3: Prosperity Crystal Meditation for Million-Dollar Abundance

Meditation is a powerful tool to connect with the energy of prosperity crystals and attract financial abundance.

Materials:

A selection of prosperity crystals (e.g., citrine, pyrite, green aventurine)

A quiet and peaceful space

Comfortable seating or cushions

Instructions:

1. Find a serene space where you can sit comfortably and be undisturbed.

2. Place the prosperity crystals in front of you, arranged in a semicircle or circle.

3. Take a few deep breaths to relax and center yourself.

4. Begin the meditation by holding one crystal in your hand. Feel its energy and visualize a golden light emanating from the crystal, filling you with the energy of prosperity.

5. As you hold each crystal, set the intention to attract a specific financial opportunity or step towards making a million dollars.

6. Close your eyes and focus on your breathing, allowing the energy of the crystals to flow through you.

7. Visualize yourself surrounded by a golden aura of prosperity, attracting financial abundance and opportunities effortlessly.

8. Stay in this meditative state for at least 15-20 minutes, allowing the energy of the prosperity crystals to align with your financial goals.

9. When you are ready, gently open your eyes and express gratitude to the crystals for their assistance.

10. Carry the energy of the meditation with you throughout the day, knowing that you are attracting the path to making a million dollars.

These practical exercises are designed to aid you in manifesting a million dollars using crystal magick. Feel free to modify these exercises as per your preferences and needs. Happy manifesting!

Chapter 5 Conclusion:

In this chapter, we delved into the enchanting realm of crystal magick for prosperity, exploring various practices to attract wealth, abundance, and financial success into our lives. Through the power of prosperity crystals, we discovered how to align our intentions with the energies of abundance, unlocking the potential of the universe to manifest our financial dreams.

From creating crystal grids to infuse our space with wealth energies to crafting crystal elixirs and carrying crystal allies for daily prosperity, we explored diverse and potent techniques to connect with the vibrational frequencies of prosperity. Each practice provided a sacred and transformative experience, empowering us to tap into the infinite possibilities of financial well-being.

Through the art of crystal decor, we learned how to transform our homes into abundant sanctuaries, inviting positive energies and attracting wealth into every corner. By harmonizing with the principles of Feng Shui and imbuing our living spaces with the energies of prosperity crystals, we created a rich tapestry of abundance that nourishes our spirits and enhances our financial opportunities.

As we embrace the magick of crystals for prosperity, we recognize that our intentions and the energy we infuse into each practice are key to unlocking the true potential of these precious gifts from the Earth. Through gratitude, trust, and belief in the power of abundance, we embrace the journey of manifesting financial success.

May the wisdom and practices shared in this chapter empower you to embrace the enchantment of crystal magick for prosperity. As you work with prosperity crystals, may they serve as powerful allies on your journey to financial abundance, guiding you towards a life of prosperity, fulfillment, and joy.

With an open heart and a magickal mindset, may you continue to weave the energies of abundance and prosperity into the very fabric of your life. Embrace the transformative energy of crystals, and may they continue to illuminate your path to financial success with radiant light and endless possibilities. Trust in the magick of prosperity crystals, and may they inspire you to live a life of abundant living and attract the financial blessings that the universe has in store for you.

Chapter 6: Tools of Prosperity Magick

This chapter introduces various tools that enhance financial magick, such as money talismans, wealth spells, and prosperity sigils. You will understand the potency of these tools and how to incorporate them into your magickal practice to amplify financial manifestations.

6.1: Understanding the Power of Money Talismans

In this chapter, we explore the fascinating world of money talismans and their significance in prosperity magick. Money talismans are powerful objects charged with specific intentions to attract wealth, success, and financial opportunities into our lives. These sacred tools have been used for centuries across different cultures and esoteric traditions to harness the energies of prosperity.

1. The Essence of Money Talismans: Money talismans are symbols or objects that carry the energy of abundance and financial success. They act as focal points for our intentions, amplifying the flow of prosperity into our lives. Common examples of money talismans include coins, specially inscribed stones or crystals, sigils, amulets, and charms.

2. Choosing the Right Money Talisman: Select a money talisman that resonates with you and your financial intentions. Some traditional talismans, such as the Four-Leaf Clover or the Chinese Lucky Cat, are popular choices for attracting luck and wealth. Alternatively, you can create a personalized talisman infused with your specific financial goals and intentions.

3. Charging and Activating the Talisman: Before using your money talisman, it is essential to charge and activate its energy. Hold the talisman in your hands and set clear intentions for the abundance and financial success you wish to attract. Visualize these intentions being infused into the talisman, imbuing it with your energy.

4. Carrying or Wearing the Talisman: Keep your charged money talisman with you at all times to maintain a constant connection with its energies. You can carry it in your wallet, pocket, or purse. Alternatively, wear it as a pendant or amulet to have it close to your heart, symbolizing your alignment with financial prosperity.

5. Rituals and Offerings: Perform regular rituals with your money talisman to reinforce its energies and strengthen your intentions. You can create a simple prosperity ritual by lighting a green or gold candle, meditating on your financial goals, and holding the talisman while visualizing abundance flowing into your life.

6. Empowering Your Talisman with Sigils: Enhance the power of your money talisman by inscribing it with prosperity sigils or symbols. Design a sigil that represents your financial desires and carve or draw it onto the talisman. This process infuses the talisman with a unique and personalized energetic signature.

7. Gratitude and Maintenance: Express gratitude to your money talisman for its assistance in attracting prosperity. Regularly cleanse and recharge the talisman to maintain its potency. You can cleanse it using smoke, running water, or visualization, and recharge it by placing it under sunlight or moonlight.

Conclusion:

Money talismans are sacred tools that serve as potent allies on our journey to financial abundance. As we embrace the power of these charged objects, we align ourselves with the frequencies of prosperity and open the gates to unlimited possibilities.

May the exploration of money talismans empower you to harness their energies and attract wealth, success, and opportunities into your life. Embrace the magick of money talismans, and may they become trusted companions, guiding you towards a life of prosperity and abundance. Trust in the power of your intentions and the energy of these sacred tools as you continue your journey towards financial prosperity with confidence and grace.

6.2: Exploring Wealth Spells and Their Potency

In this chapter, we delve into the realm of wealth spells and their potency in attracting financial abundance and prosperity. Wealth spells are magickal rituals designed to focus our intentions and energies on manifesting specific financial goals. By tapping into the ancient art of spellcasting, we can align ourselves with the flow of abundance and unlock the potential of the universe to bring forth financial success.

1. Understanding Wealth Spells: Wealth spells are rituals that combine intention, symbolism, and energy to attract prosperity into our lives. They can vary in complexity, from simple affirmations and candle spells to elaborate rituals with herbs, crystals, and other magickal tools. The key to their potency lies in the belief and focus we invest in them.

2. Setting Clear Intentions: Before performing a wealth spell, take time to clarify your financial intentions. Be specific about the goals you wish to achieve, whether it's increasing income, starting a successful business, or overcoming financial obstacles. Clear intentions help direct the energy of the spell towards your desired outcome.

3. Choosing the Right Timing: Align your wealth spell with auspicious astrological or lunar influences, if possible. For example, perform wealth spells during the waxing moon phase to attract growth and prosperity. Additionally, consider the planetary influences that correspond to financial success, such as Jupiter for expansion or Mercury for communication and opportunities.

4. Selecting Magickal Tools: Determine the magickal tools you'll use in your wealth spell based on their correspondence with prosperity and abundance. Crystals like Citrine, Pyrite, and Green Aventurine amplify wealth energies. Green or gold candles represent money and success. Herbs like cinnamon, basil, and mint symbolize prosperity. Use these tools to enhance the potency of your spell.

5. Crafting Your Wealth Spell: Design a spell that resonates with your personal beliefs and practices. You can create a simple incantation or chant, infusing it with your financial intentions. Alternatively, write your spell on a piece of paper and charge it with your energy. Be creative and authentic in crafting a spell that feels powerful to you.

6. Charging the Spell with Energy: Before casting your wealth spell, charge it with energy by meditating on your financial goals and visualizing them manifesting. Focus your intent and emotions on the successful outcome of your spell. This step charges the spell with your energy and aligns it with the flow of abundance.

7. Casting the Spell: Perform your wealth spell with sincerity and belief in its potency. Light the candles, hold the crystals, and recite the incantation with confidence. Feel the energy of the spell flowing through you and into the universe, releasing your intentions into the cosmic realm.

8. Expressing Gratitude: After casting the wealth spell, express gratitude to the universe, your spiritual guides, and the magickal energies that assisted you. Trust that your intentions are heard, and be open to receiving the abundance that comes your way.

Conclusion:

Exploring wealth spells and their potency opens the door to a realm of magick and abundance. As we engage in these sacred rituals, we align ourselves with the flow of prosperity and unlock the power of intention and belief. Wealth spells serve as transformative tools, empowering us to attract financial success and create a life of abundance.

6.3: Unleashing the Power of Prosperity Sigils

In this chapter, we explore the art of prosperity sigils and their remarkable ability to unlock the power of manifestation for financial abundance. Prosperity sigils are magickal symbols created to embody specific financial intentions, serving as gateways to the universe's limitless potential for prosperity.

1. Understanding Prosperity Sigils: Prosperity sigils are unique symbols designed to encode your financial intentions into a visual representation. These symbols bypass the conscious mind and communicate directly with the subconscious, aligning your energy with the frequencies of abundance and wealth.

2. Designing Your Prosperity Sigil: To create your prosperity sigil, start by clarifying your financial intentions. Condense your goal into a concise statement, focusing on what you wish to attract or achieve financially. Remove all vowels and repeating letters from the statement.

3. Combining Letters into a Sigil: Arrange the remaining letters from your statement into a visually appealing and cohesive symbol. You can overlap, connect, or modify the letters until your sigil takes on a unique and empowering form. Trust your intuition and allow the design to flow naturally.

4. Charging the Sigil: With your prosperity sigil complete, charge it with energy and intent. Meditate on your financial desires and visualize them as already accomplished. Imagine the energy of success flowing through you and into the sigil, infusing it with the power of manifestation.

5. Activating the Sigil: To activate the prosperity sigil, enter a magickal state of consciousness through meditation or focused concentration. Gaze at the sigil while keeping your financial intentions in mind. Allow the energy to build within you, focusing solely on the sigil's meaning.

6. Raising Energy and Releasing: When the energy reaches its peak, release it into the universe by visualizing the sigil expanding and dissolving into the cosmic energies. Let go of attachment to the outcome, trusting that the universe will respond to your intentions.

7. Hiding or Displaying the Sigil: Decide whether you want to keep your prosperity sigil hidden or display it openly. You can place it in a hidden spot, such as in your wallet or under your mattress, to work as a silent attractor of abundance. Alternatively, you can display it in your workspace or on your altar as a reminder of your financial goals.

8. Sigil Activation Frequency: For optimal potency, periodically reactivate your prosperity sigil by meditating on it and recharging it with your financial intentions. The more frequently you connect with your sigil, the more effectively it can channel your energy towards prosperity.

Conclusion:

Unleashing the power of prosperity sigils is a transformative practice that connects you to the frequencies of abundance and prosperity. As you create and activate your unique sigil, you unlock the potential of the universe to manifest your financial desires.

6.4: Embracing Abundance Rituals for Financial Magick

In this chapter, we immerse ourselves in abundance rituals for financial magick, sacred ceremonies that align us with the energies of prosperity and invite financial blessings into our lives. These rituals empower us to connect deeply with the flow of abundance, transforming our mindset and actions towards a life of financial well-being.

1. Preparation for Abundance Rituals: Before performing an abundance ritual, create a sacred and focused space. Cleanse the area with sage or incense to clear away any negative energies. Set up an altar adorned with prosperity crystals, candles, and any symbols representing wealth.

2. Prosperity Candle Ritual: Light a green or gold candle on your altar, symbolizing money and prosperity. As the flame flickers, meditate on your financial goals, visualizing them coming to fruition. Feel the energy of abundance flowing into your life. Speak affirmations of gratitude for the wealth you already possess and the prosperity on its way.

3. Abundance Crystal Grid Ritual: Create a crystal grid using prosperity crystals like Citrine, Pyrite, and Green Aventurine. Arrange the crystals in a geometric pattern on your altar or a sacred space. As you place each crystal, infuse it with your financial intentions. Activate the grid by connecting the crystals with a wand or your finger, drawing an invisible line between them. Sit within the grid, meditating on abundance and welcoming its energy into your life.

4. Prosperity Visualization Meditation: Sit or lie down in a comfortable position and close your eyes. Envision yourself surrounded by a golden light, representing the energy of abundance. Imagine money and opportunities flowing effortlessly into your life. Feel the joy and gratitude as your financial goals become a reality. Spend time in this meditative state, absorbing the feeling of prosperity.

5. Money Drawing Jar Spell: Fill a small jar with a mixture of herbs and spices associated with prosperity, such as cinnamon, basil, and mint. Add a few coins or a piece of paper with your financial intentions written on it. Seal the jar with a green or gold ribbon or wax. Hold the jar in your hands and charge it with your energy, visualizing money coming to you. Place the jar on your altar or in a special spot, and each day, hold it, meditating on abundance.

6. Full Moon Abundance Ritual: Perform this ritual during the full moon phase, a time of heightened energy for manifestation. Sit outside under the moonlight or near a window where the moon is visible. Light a white candle and dedicate it to the moon. Speak your financial intentions aloud, expressing gratitude for the abundance you seek. Bask in the moon's glow and visualize your goals becoming a reality.

7. Gratitude Jar Ritual: Obtain a jar and decorate it with symbols of prosperity or abundance. Each day, write down something you are grateful for regarding your finances. Place the notes in the jar and say a word of thanks as you do so. Over time, the jar fills with a powerful energy of gratitude, attracting more financial blessings into your life.

Conclusion:

Embracing abundance rituals for financial magick opens a portal to the vast reservoir of prosperity that surrounds us. These sacred ceremonies empower us to shift our focus, mindset, and actions towards attracting financial well-being.

6.5: Empowering Prosperity through Magickal Sigils

Within the realm of prosperity magick, sigils become the sacred symbols that hold the essence of our million-dollar aspirations. As we explore the power of prosperity sigils, we unlock the transformative potential of these magickal symbols, harnessing their energy to manifest a million-dollar fortune.

Understanding the power of money talismans and wealth spells, we recognize that sigils act as condensed forms of intention. By combining the magick of ancient symbols with our specific financial desires, we create potent sigils that serve as focal points for the universe to respond to our million-dollar dreams.

Unleashing the power of prosperity sigils requires a magickal process that begins with intention-setting and culminates in the act of charging the sigil with our energy. We infuse the sigil with our desires, fueling it with our passion and unwavering belief in the possibility of attaining a million-dollar fortune.

By embracing abundance rituals that incorporate sigils, we immerse ourselves in a magickal atmosphere that aligns our vibration with prosperity. These rituals become sacred ceremonies that honor our commitment to financial success, magnetizing us towards the wealth and abundance that the sigils represent.

As we wield the magick of prosperity sigils, we become the architects of our financial destiny. Each stroke of the symbol, each intention whispered, carries the power to transmute our desires into reality. With the universe as our canvas and our intentions as the brush, we paint the masterpiece of a million-dollar future.

But in this magickal process, we must remember that the true power of sigils lies in our intention and belief. They serve as mirrors reflecting back the essence of our desires, amplifying the energy we project into them. As we infuse the sigils with our unwavering belief in our million-dollar potential, they act as beacons that call forth the abundant blessings that await us.

In this sacred dance with prosperity sigils, we merge the ethereal and the tangible, the ancient and the modern, weaving together a magickal tapestry that leads us to financial abundance. As we gaze upon the sigils, we are reminded of our power to shape our reality, and with each gaze, the sigils beckon us closer to our million-dollar destiny.

So let the sigils be the keys that unlock the door to prosperity. With each stroke of the pen, with each charge of intention, we affirm our commitment to financial success and create a direct channel for the universe to respond.

May the magick of prosperity sigils propel us towards our million-dollar dreams, and may the universe conspire to bring forth the opportunities and blessings that align with our intentions. As we venture into the realm of million-dollar magick, may the sigils illuminate the path, guiding us with their sacred wisdom and empowering us to embrace the abundance that awaits.

6.6: Practical Exercises for Chapter 6

Exercise 1: Money Talisman Empowerment Ritual

Create and empower a powerful money talisman to attract financial abundance and opportunities on your path to making a million dollars.

Materials:

A green or gold drawstring pouch

A selection of prosperity symbols or charms (e.g., dollar signs, symbols of wealth)

A green or gold ribbon or string

A green or gold candle (for prosperity)

Anointed money-drawing oil (a blend of essential oils such as cinnamon, patchouli, and basil diluted in carrier oil)

Instructions:

1. Find a quiet and sacred space where you can perform the ritual without interruptions.

2. Cleanse and consecrate the pouch, charms, and ribbon by passing them through the smoke of the prosperity candle or sprinkling a few drops of anointed oil on them.

3. Sit comfortably with the items in front of you, and take a few deep breaths to center yourself.

4. Hold each prosperity charm or symbol in your hands, imbuing it with your million-dollar intention. Visualize each symbol attracting wealth and opportunities into your life.

5. Place the empowered charms inside the green or gold drawstring pouch.

6. Tie the pouch shut with the green or gold ribbon, sealing the energy of your intention within.

7. Hold the pouch in both hands and repeat your million-dollar affirmation or intention, infusing it with your will and energy.

8. Light the green or gold candle, representing prosperity, and let it burn throughout the ritual.

9. Hold the pouch close to the candle flame (not too close to avoid damage) and visualize the flame empowering the talisman with the fire's transformative energy.

10. When you feel the talisman is charged with energy, extinguish the candle safely.

11. Carry the talisman with you daily, whether in your pocket, purse, or on a necklace, as a constant reminder of your million-dollar intention.

Exercise 2: Prosperity Sigil Activation

Sigils are symbols charged with specific intentions. Create a prosperity sigil to focus your magickal energy on manifesting a million dollars.

Materials:

A pen and paper

A selection of prosperity symbols or imagery (optional)

A green or gold candle (for prosperity)

Instructions:

1. Find a quiet and undisturbed space to work on your prosperity sigil.

2. Take a few moments to meditate or reflect on your million-dollar goal, allowing your intentions to become clear and focused.

3. Write down your million-dollar intention in a single sentence or phrase. For example: "I am financially abundant and attract a million dollars."

4. Remove any vowels and repeating letters from the sentence to create a string of unique letters.

5. Combine the remaining letters into a visually appealing symbol or design. You can draw inspiration from prosperity symbols or create your own based on your intuition.

6. Meditate on the sigil, charging it with your intention and energy. Visualize the sigil glowing with green or gold light, radiating the energy of prosperity.

7. If desired, create a larger version of the sigil on a separate piece of paper, adding prosperity symbols or imagery around it.

8. Place the larger sigil in front of the green or gold prosperity candle and let it burn for a few minutes, infusing the sigil with the candle's energy.

9. Carry the smaller sigil with you or place it in a prominent location where you can see it daily, reinforcing your million-dollar intention.

Exercise 3: Abundance Ritual with Financial Planning

Combine the magickal power of intention with practical financial planning to manifest a million dollars.

Materials:

A green or gold cloth

A selection of prosperity crystals (e.g., citrine, green aventurine, pyrite)

A green or gold candle (for prosperity)

A notebook and pen

Financial planning tools (e.g., budgeting apps, spreadsheets)

Instructions:

1. Set up your sacred space with the green or gold cloth as a representation of abundance.

2. Place the prosperity crystals in a circle or semicircle around the green or gold candle.

3. Light the candle, symbolizing the illumination of your financial path.

4. Sit comfortably with your notebook and pen, ready to combine magick with practical planning.

5. Take a few deep breaths to center yourself and clear your mind.

6. Hold the prosperity crystals in your hands and set your million-dollar intention. Visualize yourself achieving financial success, making a million dollars, and managing it wisely.

7. Begin the financial planning process by reviewing your current financial situation. Take note of your income, expenses, debts, and investments.

8. Set specific financial goals and milestones to help you progress towards making a million dollars.

9. Create a practical budget that aligns with your financial goals and includes a dedicated allocation for saving and investing.

10. As you work on your financial plan, periodically pause to connect with the energy of the prosperity crystals, infusing your financial decisions with magickal intention.

11. Once your financial plan is in place, close the ritual by expressing gratitude to the universe, your guides, and the prosperity crystals for their assistance.

12. Follow through with your financial plan, reviewing and adjusting it as needed to keep your million-dollar journey on track.

These practical exercises incorporate the use of crystals, sigils, and practical financial planning to align your intentions and actions with your financial goals. Remember, consistency and belief in your magickal practices are key to achieving your desired outcomes. Good luck on your magickal journey to financial abundance!

Chapter 6 Conclusion:

In this chapter, we delved into the enchanting world of prosperity magick and the powerful tools that empower us to attract abundance and financial blessings into our lives. From money talismans and prosperity sigils to abundance rituals and wealth spells, we explored a wide array of sacred practices that align us with the energies of prosperity.

Through the art of intention, belief, and focused energy, we discovered the transformative potential of these magickal tools. Each practice serves as a gateway to the flow of abundance, guiding us on a path of financial well-being and success.

As we embrace the magick of prosperity tools, we recognize the importance of clarity in our financial intentions. By setting clear goals and connecting deeply with the energies of prosperity, we align ourselves with the universe's infinite possibilities for abundance.

May the exploration of prosperity magick inspire you to cultivate a magickal mindset and embrace the transformative power of intention and belief. Trust in the energies of these sacred tools, and may they become steadfast allies on your journey towards financial prosperity.

As you continue your magickal journey, may you walk confidently and gracefully on the path of abundance, attracting wealth, success, and opportunities with every step you take. Embrace the magick of prosperity, and may it weave its transformative energies into every aspect of your life, guiding you towards a life of financial abundance and fulfillment.

With a heart full of gratitude and an unwavering belief in the power of prosperity magick, may you manifest your financial dreams and co-create a reality brimming with prosperity and joy.

Chapter 7: Lunar Magick for Financial Cycles

The moon has a significant impact on financial rhythms, and this chapter explores its influence on financial cycles. You will learn how to align your financial intentions with the different phases of the moon, such as seeding intentions during the New Moon, cultivating growth during the Waxing Moon, harvesting abundance during the Full Moon, and releasing blocks during the Waning Moon. The chapter also covers the Blue Moon and Lunar Eclipse as opportunities for magickal transformation.

7.1: The Moon's Influence on Financial Rhythms

In this chapter, we explore the captivating realm of lunar magick and its profound impact on financial cycles. The moon, with its ever-changing phases, has long been revered as a potent source of energy that influences various aspects of our lives, including our financial well-being. By aligning our financial practices with the lunar cycles, we can harness the moon's power to enhance our prosperity and abundance.

1. The Moon's Phases and Financial Energy: The moon cycles through eight distinct phases, each holding unique energies that correspond to different stages of growth, release, and manifestation. Understanding the significance of each phase can help us navigate our financial journey with greater wisdom and intention.

New Moon: The new moon represents new beginnings and is an opportune time to set financial intentions and goals for the upcoming lunar cycle. It is a period of planting the seeds of prosperity and envisioning the financial outcomes we desire.

Waxing Moon: As the moon waxes, its energy amplifies, making it an excellent time for taking action towards our financial goals. This is a phase of growth and expansion, where we can focus on increasing our income, seeking new opportunities, and making investments.

Full Moon: The full moon is a powerful time for harvesting the results of our financial efforts. It illuminates our financial situation, highlighting what is working well and what needs adjustment. It is also an ideal time for releasing financial blocks and expressing gratitude for our current abundance.

Waning Moon: During the waning moon, the energy is conducive to letting go of what no longer serves our financial goals. It is a phase of release and purification, making it an excellent time to pay off debts, clear clutter, and reassess financial strategies.

2. Lunar Rituals for Financial Intentions: Aligning our financial intentions with the moon's phases can be amplified through lunar rituals. During the new moon, perform a ritual to set clear financial intentions and visualize your goals. Use the waxing moon to take inspired action towards your financial plans, and on the full moon, express gratitude for your current abundance. During the waning moon, perform rituals to release financial blocks and make space for new opportunities.

3. Moon Phase Timing for Financial Decisions: Consider the moon's phase when making significant financial decisions. During the waxing moon, when energies are building, it is an auspicious time to sign contracts, negotiate deals, or seek new financial ventures. During the waning moon, exercise caution and focus on reviewing your finances, paying off debts, and refraining from impulsive spending.

4. Creating a Lunar Financial Journal: Keep a lunar financial journal to track your financial progress throughout the moon's phases. Record your financial intentions during the new moon, actions taken during the waxing moon, results and insights during the full moon, and areas of release and improvement during the waning moon. This journal can provide valuable insights into your financial journey and help you make informed decisions.

Conclusion:

Lunar magick for financial cycles is a transformative practice that aligns us with the natural rhythms of the moon and its influence on our financial journey. By understanding and harnessing the energies of each moon phase, we can amplify our financial intentions, take inspired actions, release limiting beliefs, and manifest greater prosperity and abundance.

7.2: The New Moon: Seeding Financial Intentions

In the realm of lunar magick, the new moon stands as a potent and fertile time for seeding financial intentions and planting the seeds of abundance. As the moon begins its monthly cycle anew, it presents a powerful opportunity to set clear and focused financial goals, aligning our intentions with the universal energies of growth and manifestation.

1. Embracing the Blank Canvas: The new moon signifies a fresh start, providing us with a blank canvas to draw our financial dreams upon. Embrace this moment of renewal and allow yourself to release any past financial challenges or limitations. By doing so, you open yourself to new possibilities and the potential of manifesting a more prosperous reality.

2. Setting Clear Financial Intentions: During the new moon, take time to reflect on your financial aspirations and desires. What are your short-term and long-term financial goals? Be specific and precise in defining what you wish to achieve. Write down your intentions in a journal or on a piece of paper, infusing each word with the energy of abundance.

3. Visualization and Vision Boarding: Utilize the power of visualization to amplify your financial intentions. Close your eyes and envision your financial goals as already accomplished. See yourself living a life of abundance and financial freedom. You can also create a vision board by collecting images, words, and symbols that represent your financial dreams, and arrange them on a board or paper. Place the vision board in a visible spot to reinforce your intentions daily.

4. Moonlight Meditation and Ritual: Under the glow of the new moon, find a quiet space to meditate on your financial intentions. Light a white or silver candle to symbolize the moon's energy. Hold your written intentions or vision board in your hands, and with focused intent, speak your financial goals aloud. Feel the moon's energy supporting and amplifying your intentions.

5. Charging Crystals for Financial Intentions: Harness the energy of prosperity crystals by charging them during the new moon. Place crystals like Citrine, Pyrite, and Green Aventurine on a windowsill or outdoors where they can absorb the moonlight. As you do so, visualize the crystals becoming potent allies in manifesting your financial desires.

6. Gratitude and Trust: Express gratitude to the new moon for this fresh start and for the abundance that is on its way. Trust that the universe is aligning with your financial intentions and will support you in your journey towards prosperity.

Conclusion:

The new moon is a potent time for seeding financial intentions and setting the stage for growth and abundance. By embracing the energy of renewal and aligning with the lunar cycle, we can tap into the natural rhythms of the universe to manifest our financial goals.

7.3: The Waxing Moon: Cultivating Growth and Prosperity

As the moon begins its ascent from the new moon towards its fullness, it enters the waxing phase, a time of increased energy and growth. During this lunar period, the waxing moon lends its powerful influence to our financial endeavors, making it an ideal time to take inspired actions towards cultivating prosperity and abundance.

1. Harnessing the Energy of Growth: The waxing moon amplifies our intentions and actions, offering a surge of energy that propels us towards our financial goals. As we harness this growth-oriented energy, we can focus on increasing our income, attracting new opportunities, and expanding our financial resources.

2. Taking Inspired Financial Actions: During the waxing moon, take deliberate and inspired actions aligned with your financial intentions. Seek new avenues to increase your earnings, explore investment opportunities, or expand your professional network. Be open to new possibilities and trust your intuition as you make financial decisions.

3. Charging Money Talismans and Crystals: Empower your money talismans and prosperity crystals during the waxing moon. Hold your money talisman or financial amulet in your hands, visualizing it absorbing the moon's energy and amplifying your prosperity intentions. Similarly, charge your prosperity crystals under the moonlight, infusing them with the energy of growth and financial abundance.

4. Money Visualization Meditation: Engage in a money visualization meditation during the waxing moon phase. Find a quiet space, close your eyes, and visualize yourself surrounded by a golden light of prosperity. Imagine money flowing to you effortlessly and opportunities blossoming in abundance. Feel the excitement and joy as you witness your financial goals materializing.

5. Affirmations for Prosperity: During the waxing moon, incorporate affirmations into your daily routine to reinforce your belief in financial abundance. Repeat positive statements such as "I am worthy of financial success," "Opportunities for wealth come to me easily," and "I am open to receiving prosperity in all areas of my life." Let these affirmations strengthen your mindset and attract prosperity into your reality.

6. Gratitude for Growing Abundance: Express gratitude during the waxing moon for the growing abundance in your life. Acknowledge the progress you've made towards your financial goals and be thankful for the opportunities that have presented themselves. Gratitude opens the heart to receive even more blessings.

Conclusion:

The waxing moon is a time of vibrant energy and growth, making it an opportune phase for cultivating prosperity and abundance. By aligning our actions with the moon's waxing energy, we can take inspired steps towards manifesting our financial desires and embracing the flow of abundance.

7.4: The Full Moon: Harvesting Financial Abundance

The full moon is a powerful and illuminating phase of the lunar cycle. As the moon reaches its peak brightness, it bestows its radiant light upon us, revealing insights and opportunities related to our financial well-being. This phase presents a potent time for harvesting the results of our financial efforts, expressing gratitude, and releasing any blocks to abundance.

1. Illumination and Clarity: The full moon shines a light on our financial situation, providing clarity and insight into our progress and achievements. It is a time to assess our financial goals, review our strategies, and celebrate the successes we've achieved thus far. Take time to reflect on the positive outcomes and growth you've experienced in your financial journey.

2. Gratitude and Abundance: Express deep gratitude for the abundance in your life during the full moon. Acknowledge the financial blessings you've received and the prosperity that surrounds you. Gratitude opens the heart to receive even more abundance, inviting the universe to shower you with its riches.

3. Releasing Limiting Beliefs: Use the full moon's energy to release any limiting beliefs or financial blocks that may be holding you back. Write down any negative thoughts or fears related to money and prosperity, and then burn or bury the paper as a symbolic act of releasing those limitations. Replace these beliefs with positive affirmations of financial abundance and self-worth.

4. Full Moon Prosperity Ritual: Perform a full moon prosperity ritual to honor the abundance in your life and to attract even more prosperity. Light a white or silver candle to represent the moon's energy and set up your sacred space with prosperity crystals and symbols. Take time to meditate on the financial goals you wish to achieve and visualize them as already accomplished. Release your intentions into the universe, trusting that the full moon will amplify their manifestation.

5. Financial Review and Adjustments: During the full moon, review your financial goals and strategies. Assess the areas where you've succeeded and those that may require adjustments. Use this time to make informed financial decisions and set new intentions for the upcoming lunar cycle.

6. Moonlit Gratitude Walk: Take a moonlit gratitude walk on the night of the full moon. Step outside and bask in the moon's glow, appreciating the beauty and abundance of the natural world. With each step, express gratitude for the financial blessings in your life and the opportunities that lie ahead.

Conclusion:

The full moon is a time of illumination, gratitude, and manifestation in the realm of financial magick. By embracing the full moon's energy, we can gain clarity on our financial journey, express gratitude for our current abundance, and release any limiting beliefs that may hinder our progress.

7.5: The Waning Moon: Releasing Financial Blocks

As the moon transitions from its fullness towards the new moon, it enters the waning phase, a period of release and purification. During the waning moon, we have the opportunity to let go of anything that no longer serves our financial goals and to release any blockages that may be hindering our abundance.

1. Letting Go and Releasing: The waning moon invites us to release and let go of financial habits, beliefs, and situations that no longer align with our prosperity goals. This phase empowers us to shed limiting mindsets and negative thought patterns that might be preventing us from attracting the financial abundance we desire.

2. Financial Detoxification: Use the waning moon as a time for financial detoxification. Review your financial decisions and expenses, identifying any unnecessary spending or debt that you can release. Consider decluttering your financial space and organizing your financial records to create clarity and abundance.

3. Emotional Healing for Abundance: Emotional healing is vital for attracting abundance. Take time during the waning moon to reflect on any emotional attachments or fears related to money. Journal your thoughts and emotions, allowing yourself to release any negative associations with money and embrace a healthier relationship with abundance.

4. Releasing Financial Burdens: If you have financial debts or obligations, use the waning moon to focus on paying them off or finding practical solutions to alleviate the burden. Seek financial advice or create a budget to manage your finances more effectively.

5. Forgiveness for Financial Peace: Forgiveness is a powerful act of releasing emotional and financial burdens. Forgive yourself for past financial mistakes and let go of any resentment towards others related to money matters. Forgiveness creates space for positive financial energy to flow.

6. Waning Moon Ritual of Release: Perform a waning moon ritual of release to let go of financial blocks and limitations. Light a black or dark blue candle to represent the waning moon's energy of release. Write down any financial blocks or negative beliefs on a piece of paper. As you burn the paper, visualize those blockages dissipating, leaving space for abundance to flow freely.

Conclusion:

The waning moon is a time of cleansing, purification, and release in the realm of financial magick. By embracing this phase, we can let go of what no longer serves our financial goals and create space for new opportunities and abundance.

7.6: The Blue Moon: Amplifying Magickal Opportunities

The rare and enchanting Blue Moon is an extraordinary lunar event that occurs when there are two full moons within a single calendar month. This celestial occurrence presents a unique and potent opportunity to amplify our financial intentions and harness the magickal energies of abundance.

1. Embracing the Magick of the Blue Moon: The Blue Moon is a special time of amplified energy and manifestation. Embrace this celestial event as a powerful portal for magnifying your financial intentions and attracting abundance into your life. It is a moment of heightened magickal potential.

2. Setting Blue Moon Intentions: As the Blue Moon approaches, take time to set special financial intentions that you wish to manifest during this magickal time. Write down your most cherished financial desires and goals, infusing them with strong emotion and belief.

3. Blue Moon Ritual and Meditation: On the night of the Blue Moon, create a sacred space and perform a ritual or meditation to honor this auspicious event. Light blue candles and use crystals associated with abundance, such as Blue Apatite, Selenite, or Labradorite. Visualize your financial intentions with utmost clarity, feeling the magickal energy of the Blue Moon amplifying your desires.

4. Engaging in Abundance Practices: During the Blue Moon, engage in abundance practices that resonate with you. This could include giving to charity, performing acts of kindness, or sharing your wealth and knowledge with others. As you give, the universe responds with even greater blessings.

5. Blue Moon Tarot or Oracle Reading: Seek guidance from divination tools like tarot or oracle cards during the Blue Moon. Use these magickal tools to gain insights into your financial journey, uncover hidden opportunities, and receive guidance on how to proceed towards prosperity.

6. Gratitude for the Abundance: Express profound gratitude during the Blue Moon for the abundance in your life. Be thankful for the financial blessings you've received, as well as the ones that are on their way. Gratitude opens the door for even more abundance to flow into your reality.

Conclusion:

The Blue Moon is a celestial gift of amplified energy and magickal opportunities. By embracing this rare event, we can enhance our financial intentions and attract abundance into our lives with greater potency.

7.7: The Lunar Eclipse: Illuminating Financial Transformation

The lunar eclipse is a captivating celestial event that occurs when the Earth comes between the sun and the moon, casting a shadow over the moon's surface. This potent lunar phenomenon symbolizes transformation and renewal. During a lunar eclipse, the moon's energy is intensified, offering a profound opportunity for inner reflection and financial growth.

1. Embracing the Energy of Transformation: The lunar eclipse heralds a period of profound transformation and change. Embrace this time as an invitation to explore your financial beliefs, behaviors, and goals. Use the lunar eclipse's energy to illuminate any areas of your financial life that require transformation and improvement.

2. Inner Reflection and Introspection: During a lunar eclipse, turn your focus inward and engage in deep introspection regarding your financial journey. Reflect on your financial choices, values, and aspirations. Be honest with yourself about any patterns or habits that may be hindering your financial growth.

3. Releasing Old Patterns and Beliefs: The lunar eclipse presents an opportune moment to release old patterns and limiting beliefs surrounding money. Write down any negative thought patterns or self-doubts related to your finances. As the eclipse passes, burn or bury the paper as a symbolic act of releasing these limitations.

4. Lunar Eclipse Ritual of Transformation: Perform a lunar eclipse ritual to embrace the energy of transformation and renewal. Create a sacred space with candles and crystals to amplify the eclipse's energy. Meditate on your financial intentions, visualizing the energy of the eclipse purifying and transforming any stagnant or negative financial energy.

5. Seek Guidance and Clarity: Utilize divination tools such as tarot cards or oracle cards during the lunar eclipse to seek guidance and clarity on your financial path. These tools can offer valuable insights into the changes and opportunities that may arise in your financial journey.

6. Embrace Change with Openness: The lunar eclipse often brings unexpected changes and opportunities. Embrace these shifts with openness and trust that they are leading you towards greater financial alignment and growth. Stay adaptable and open to new possibilities that may present themselves during this transformative time.

Conclusion:

The lunar eclipse is a time of profound transformation and illumination in the realm of financial magick. By embracing this celestial event, we can delve into our financial journey with introspection and openness to change.

7.8: The Cosmic Eclipse of Financial Transformation

In the cosmic symphony of financial cycles, the lunar eclipse emerges as a pivotal moment of profound transformation. As we explore the magick of the lunar eclipse for financial metamorphosis, we unlock the gateway to making a million dollars with the universe's unwavering support.

The lunar eclipse becomes the celestial phenomenon that casts its illuminating light upon our financial journey. As the moon aligns with the sun and the earth, we stand in the shadow of cosmic energies that challenge us to release old patterns and embrace new possibilities.

Harnessing the power of the lunar eclipse, we embrace the art of illuminating financial transformation. Just as the moon unveils itself in a celestial dance of light and shadow, we, too, confront the shadows that hold us back from our million-dollar potential.

In the lunar eclipse's embrace, we release financial blocks and limiting beliefs that no longer serve our aspirations. With each step towards self-awareness and introspection, we shed the layers of doubt, fear, and scarcity, allowing the light of abundance to penetrate our beings.

As we immerse ourselves in the transformative energy of the lunar eclipse, we align with the cosmic forces that guide us towards making a million dollars. The eclipse serves as a catalyst for change, igniting a magickal metamorphosis that propels us towards financial success.

But amidst this profound cosmic dance, we must remember that the lunar eclipse is a time for contemplation and inner work. It calls us to examine our relationship with money and to confront any self-imposed limitations that hinder our financial growth.

During this celestial event, we embrace the opportunity to set new intentions, infusing them with the transformative energy of the lunar eclipse. With unwavering determination, we anchor our million-dollar aspirations in the cosmic currents, trusting that the universe will respond to our magickal call.

In this magickal communion with the lunar eclipse, we become the conscious co-creators of our financial destiny. We surrender to the universal flow, allowing the cosmic eclipse to guide us towards the million-dollar potential that resides within.

As the shadow passes and the light returns, we emerge from the lunar eclipse with newfound clarity and purpose. We are ready to embark on the next phase of our financial journey, transformed and empowered by the cosmic energies that have guided us.

With each lunar eclipse, we embrace the cycle of financial transformation, knowing that the universe's support is unwavering. As we step into the light of our million-dollar aspirations, we stand as living proof that the magick of the lunar eclipse has illuminated our path to financial abundance.

So let the lunar eclipse be the celestial guide that leads us towards making a million dollars. With each cosmic alignment, with each introspective moment, we align ourselves with the universe's grand plan for financial prosperity.

May the magick of the lunar eclipse awaken our highest potential, and may the shadows that once clouded our path be replaced with the radiant light of financial abundance. As we journey through the cosmic eclipse of financial transformation, may we embrace the unfolding magick and step into the million-dollar reality that awaits us.

7.9: Practical Exercises for Chapter 7

Exercise 1: New Moon Million-Dollar Intention Setting

Harness the powerful energy of the New Moon to set clear intentions for making a million dollars and initiating new financial opportunities.

Materials:

A quiet and comfortable space

A green or gold candle (for prosperity)

A journal or notebook

A green or gold pen

Instructions:

1. Find a peaceful space where you can sit comfortably and observe the New Moon's energy.

2. Light the green or gold candle to symbolize prosperity and financial growth.

3. Take a few deep breaths to center yourself and focus on your million-dollar intention.

4. Write down your financial goals and aspirations in your journal, starting with the statement: "I am making a million dollars through magick and intention."

5. Be specific about how you plan to achieve this goal. Include details about your sources of income, investments, business ventures, or any other means you intend to use.

6. Spend some time visualizing yourself already achieving your million-dollar goal. See yourself living a life of financial abundance and fulfillment.

7. Repeat your million-dollar intention aloud, infusing it with passion and belief.

8. Close your eyes and meditate, feeling the New Moon's energy supporting your intention and amplifying your magickal desire.

9. After the meditation, blow out the candle, symbolizing the initiation of your million-dollar journey.

10. Over the coming weeks, revisit your journal, review your intention, and take inspired actions towards your financial goals. Use the New Moon phase each month to renew your commitment and focus on making a million dollars.

Exercise 2: Full Moon Prosperity Visualization

Utilize the Full Moon's potent energy to magnify your financial prosperity visualization and amplify your intentions of making a million dollars.

Materials:

A quiet and dimly lit space

A green or gold cloth

A selection of prosperity crystals (e.g., citrine, green aventurine, pyrite)

A green or gold candle (for prosperity)

A vision board or images representing your million-dollar financial success

Instructions:

1. Set up your sacred space with the green or gold cloth to create an ambiance of abundance.

2. Place the prosperity crystals in a circle or semicircle around the green or gold candle.

3. Light the candle to invoke the Full Moon's energy of illumination and manifestation.

4. Sit comfortably in front of the candle and crystals, taking a few deep breaths to relax and center yourself.

5. Hold the prosperity crystals in your hands, infusing them with your million-dollar intention. Visualize each crystal radiating green or gold light, amplifying your prosperity energies.

6. If you have a vision board or images representing your financial goals, focus on them to intensify your visualization.

7. Close your eyes and begin your Full Moon prosperity visualization. See yourself as a magnet for wealth and opportunities, already experiencing financial success, and making a million dollars.

8. Engage all your senses in the visualization, feeling the joy, gratitude, and fulfillment that come with achieving your financial dreams.

9. Spend at least 10-15 minutes in this visualization, immersing yourself fully in the energy of prosperity and abundance.

10. When you feel complete, express gratitude to the Full Moon and the prosperity crystals for their assistance.

11. Repeat this visualization practice during each Full Moon phase to maintain your focus on your financial goals and strengthen your manifestation power.

Exercise 3: Lunar Eclipse Transformation Ritual

During a Lunar Eclipse, tap into the transformative energy to release financial blocks and old patterns that may hinder your path to making a million dollars.

Materials:

A quiet and sacred space

A black or purple cloth

A selection of cleansing and releasing herbs (e.g., sage, lavender)

A black or purple candle (for transformation)

A piece of paper and a pen

Instructions:

1. Prepare your sacred space with the black or purple cloth, representing the transformative energy of the Lunar Eclipse.

2. Light the black or purple candle, invoking the energy of transformation and release.

3. Take a few deep breaths to center yourself and focus on your financial goals.

4. Use the cleansing herbs to smudge yourself and the space, purifying and releasing any negative or stagnant energies.

5. Sit comfortably with the paper and pen, ready to release any financial blocks or limiting beliefs.

6. Write down any fears, doubts, or old patterns that may be holding you back from making a million dollars. Be honest and open with yourself.

7. Take a moment to acknowledge these blocks and understand that they no longer serve you.

8. Visualize the Lunar Eclipse's shadow passing over your paper, symbolizing the release of these financial blocks.

9. Tear the paper into small pieces, and as you do so, repeat a releasing affirmation such as: "I release these blocks and make way for financial abundance."

10. Light the torn pieces of paper with the candle flame, allowing them to burn safely in a heatproof container. As they burn, visualize the negative energies being transformed and released into the universe.

11. Close the ritual by expressing gratitude to the Lunar Eclipse and the transformative energy it brought.

12. In the days following the Lunar Eclipse, pay attention to any shifts or opportunities that present themselves. Embrace the energy of transformation and take inspired actions towards your million-dollar goal.

The practical exercises for Chapter 7 focus on making a million dollars through lunar magick. These exercises utilize the New Moon, Full Moon, and Lunar Eclipse energies to set intentions, amplify prosperity visualizations, and release financial blocks. Remember to practice these exercises regularly and trust in the magickal energies to support your journey towards financial abundance. Good luck on your path to making a million dollars!

Chapter 7 Conclusion:

In the exploration of lunar magick for financial cycles, we have embarked on a journey of aligning with the powerful energies of the moon to enhance our financial well-being. Each phase of the lunar cycle offers a unique opportunity for manifestation, release, and transformation in the realm of abundance and prosperity.

From the seeding of financial intentions during the new moon to the harvesting of abundance under the full moon's glow, we have learned to embrace the ebb and flow of lunar energies in our financial endeavors. The waxing moon fuels our growth and motivation, while the waning moon empowers us to release limitations and negative beliefs. The Blue Moon and lunar eclipse provide rare and potent opportunities for amplifying magickal intentions and igniting inner transformation.

Through rituals, meditation, gratitude, and the use of magickal tools, we have connected with the moon's energies, strengthening our financial manifestations and empowering our intentions. The lunar cycle has served as a guide, reminding us of the interconnectedness between the universe and our financial journey.

As we continue to walk the path of lunar magick for financial cycles, let us remember that our intentions, actions, and beliefs shape our financial reality. By embracing the energy of each lunar phase and aligning with the natural rhythms of the cosmos, we can create a harmonious dance of abundance and prosperity in our lives.

May the wisdom and magick of lunar cycles always guide us towards financial growth, transformation, and illumination. Embrace the ever-changing moon as a cosmic ally on your journey towards financial prosperity, and may its luminous energy continue to bless your path with abundance and success.

Trust in the lunar magick and the universe's response as you move forward with confidence and grace, knowing that you are a co-creator of your financial destiny. May your financial journey be filled with lunar blessings, and may you thrive in the ever-present flow of abundance.

Chapter 8: Practical Prosperity Tips

This chapter provides practical tips to integrate financial magick into everyday life. You will learn how to use affirmations for financial abundance, practice gratitude to enhance wealth consciousness, incorporate money magick in daily routines, empower yourself financially through budgeting and planning, and consider ethical aspects in your financial magick practice.

8.1: Affirmations for Financial Abundance

Affirmations are powerful statements that can help reprogram your subconscious mind and shift your beliefs about money and abundance. By consistently affirming positive statements related to financial abundance, you can attract prosperity into your life and cultivate a mindset of wealth consciousness.

1. Choose Empowering Affirmations: Select affirmations that resonate with you and align with your financial goals. Examples of empowering affirmations include:

"I am worthy of financial abundance and success."

"Money flows to me effortlessly and abundantly."

"I attract prosperity in all areas of my life."

"I am a magnet for wealth and opportunities."

2. Repetition and Belief: Repeat your affirmations daily with conviction and belief. The more you affirm these statements, the more they become ingrained in your subconscious mind, guiding your thoughts and actions towards financial abundance.

3. Visualization with Affirmations: Combine visualization with affirmations for even greater impact. As you repeat your affirmations, vividly imagine yourself living the life of abundance you desire. Visualize your financial goals as already accomplished and experience the emotions of success and fulfillment.

4. Morning and Evening Affirmation Routine: Incorporate affirmations into your morning and evening routines. Start your day by affirming your financial intentions, setting a positive tone for the day ahead. Before sleep, reaffirm your beliefs in abundance, allowing your subconscious mind to work on attracting prosperity while you rest.

5. Affirmations for Specific Goals: Tailor affirmations to address specific financial goals or challenges you may be facing. For instance:

"I easily pay off all my debts and become financially free."

"I attract lucrative opportunities that align with my passions."

"My investments grow and multiply, securing my financial future."

6. Gratitude Affirmations: Combine gratitude with affirmations to amplify their potency. Express gratitude for the financial blessings you have received and those that are on their way. Gratitude enhances your positive energy and attracts more abundance into your life.

7. Record Affirmations: Record your affirmations in your own voice and listen to them regularly. Hearing your affirmations from your own voice strengthens the impact and reinforces your beliefs in financial abundance.

Conclusion:

Affirmations are an invaluable tool in your journey towards financial prosperity. By choosing and repeating empowering statements, you can shift your mindset, attract abundance, and create a positive relationship with money. Embrace the practice of affirmations with consistency and belief, and watch as your financial reality aligns with your abundant intentions.

8.2: Gratitude Practice for Wealth Consciousness

Gratitude is a transformative practice that can profoundly shift your mindset and attract more abundance into your life. By cultivating a consistent gratitude practice, you open the door to wealth consciousness and invite more financial blessings into your reality.

1. Daily Gratitude Journal: Start a daily gratitude journal dedicated to your financial journey. Each day, write down at least three things you are grateful for regarding money, wealth, or financial opportunities. Acknowledge even the smallest financial blessings, as they contribute to a mindset of abundance.

2. Gratitude Affirmations: Combine gratitude with affirmations to amplify their impact. Include statements such as:

"I am grateful for the financial abundance flowing into my life."

"I appreciate the opportunities that bring prosperity into my path."

"I am thankful for the money I have and the money that comes to me effortlessly."

3. Gratitude Meditation: Incorporate a gratitude meditation into your daily routine. Find a quiet space, close your eyes, and focus on the feeling of gratitude. Visualize yourself surrounded by a golden light of abundance, and immerse yourself in the sensations of thankfulness for the financial blessings in your life.

4. Express Gratitude for Challenges: Practice gratitude even during financial challenges. Instead of dwelling on difficulties, focus on the lessons they offer and the potential for growth. Gratitude in challenging times opens the way for solutions and new opportunities to arise.

5. Share the Gift of Giving: Give back to others and your community as a gesture of gratitude for your financial abundance. Contributing to charities, supporting causes, or helping those in need cultivates a sense of abundance and reinforces the flow of prosperity in your life.

6. Appreciate Non-Material Wealth: Gratitude extends beyond material possessions. Acknowledge and appreciate the non-material aspects of wealth, such as love, health, relationships, and personal growth. Recognize the richness of your life in all its forms.

7. Gratitude Visualization: Incorporate gratitude visualization into your daily routine. As you go about your day, visualize your financial goals already achieved. Express deep gratitude for the prosperity you have received and the abundance that is unfolding in your life.

Conclusion:

A gratitude practice is a transformative key to wealth consciousness. By embracing gratitude, you shift your focus from scarcity to abundance, attracting more financial blessings into your life. Embrace gratitude as a way of life, and let it guide you on your journey towards financial success and fulfillment.

8.3: Money Magick in Daily Life

Money magick is not limited to elaborate rituals or specific practices. It can be seamlessly integrated into your daily life, infusing your actions and mindset with the energy of abundance and prosperity. Embrace the following money magick practices to create a positive and prosperous relationship with money in your everyday existence.

1. Conscious Spending: Practice mindful spending by being intentional with your purchases. Before making a financial decision, ask yourself if the purchase aligns with your financial goals and values. Avoid impulsive buying and focus on investing in items that add value to your life.

2. Abundance Affirmations: Throughout the day, silently repeat abundance affirmations in your mind. Use statements like "I attract money easily," "I am financially secure," or "I am a magnet for wealth." Affirmations will rewire your thoughts and attract more financial opportunities.

3. Money Sigils: Create simple money sigils to infuse your financial intentions into everyday objects. Draw or inscribe symbols of abundance on your wallet, financial documents, or personal items to magnify the energy of prosperity in your life.

4. Blessing Your Money: Before using money, take a moment to bless it with gratitude and positivity. Acknowledge money as a tool for abundance and affirm that it will multiply and flow back to you in greater measure.

5. Giving and Receiving: Embrace the cycle of giving and receiving in your interactions with money. Be generous when you can, and receive with gratitude when others offer financial gifts or opportunities.

6. Financial Visualization: Visualize your financial goals coming to fruition during idle moments or while meditating. See yourself celebrating financial success and feeling the emotions of abundance and achievement.

7. Appreciating Abundance: Take time daily to appreciate the abundance already present in your life. Focus on the positive aspects of your finances and express gratitude for the money you have.

8. Charging Daily Objects: Charge objects you frequently use, such as your computer, phone, or work tools, with prosperity energy. Hold the intention that these objects will assist you in attracting financial opportunities.

9. Abundance Rituals: Incorporate small abundance rituals into your daily routine, such as lighting a green candle or using essential oils associated with prosperity. These rituals will reinforce your intentions and create a magickal environment of abundance.

Conclusion:

Money magick in daily life allows you to harness the power of abundance seamlessly and consistently. By infusing your everyday actions and mindset with prosperity energy, you create a positive relationship with money and invite financial opportunities into your life.

8.4: Financial Empowerment through Budgeting and Planning

Budgeting and financial planning are essential tools for achieving financial empowerment and prosperity. When you take control of your finances through mindful budgeting and strategic planning, you set yourself on the path to long-term financial success and abundance.

1. Assess Your Financial Situation: Begin by assessing your current financial situation. Analyze your income, expenses, debts, and assets. This evaluation will provide clarity on where you stand financially and areas that require attention.

2. Create a Realistic Budget: Craft a detailed budget that aligns with your financial goals and values. Allocate your income into categories such as essentials, savings, investments, and discretionary spending. Stick to your budget diligently, ensuring you spend within your means.

3. Set Financial Goals: Establish clear and achievable financial goals. Define short-term, medium-term, and long-term objectives. Having specific goals will provide direction and motivation for your financial journey.

4. Track Your Spending: Keep track of every expenditure to maintain awareness of your financial habits. Tracking expenses helps identify areas where you can cut back and save more money for your goals.

5. Build an Emergency Fund: Prioritize building an emergency fund to handle unexpected expenses without derailing your financial plans. Having a safety net brings peace of mind and financial stability.

6. Reduce Debt Strategically: If you have debts, create a plan to pay them off strategically. Focus on high-interest debts first, while making minimum payments on others. As you clear debts, redirect the funds to accelerate your progress.

7. Invest for Growth: Explore investment opportunities that align with your risk tolerance and financial goals. Investments have the potential to grow your wealth over time and provide financial security for the future.

8. Review and Adjust Regularly: Regularly review your budget and financial plan to ensure they remain relevant and effective. Life circumstances change, and adapting your financial strategy accordingly is essential for continued progress.

9. Financial Visualization and Gratitude: Combine budgeting and planning with financial visualization and gratitude. Visualize yourself achieving your financial goals and feel the emotions of success. Express gratitude for your financial blessings and the progress you make.

10. Seek Professional Advice: If needed, seek advice from financial professionals or advisors. Their expertise can provide valuable insights and strategies for optimizing your financial situation.

Conclusion:

Budgeting and financial planning are powerful tools that empower you to take control of your finances and shape your financial destiny. When coupled with prosperity practices and a positive mindset, you create a foundation for lasting financial abundance.

8.5: Ethical Considerations in Financial Magick

While harnessing the power of financial magick, it is essential to approach this practice with a sense of ethics and responsibility. Magick should never be used to harm others or manipulate financial situations for personal gain. Instead, align your financial magick with ethical principles to promote harmony, fairness, and positive outcomes for everyone involved.

1. The Law of Threefold Return: Understand the Law of Threefold Return, which states that whatever energy or intention you put out into the universe will return to you threefold. This principle reminds us to act with integrity and avoid using financial magick for harmful purposes.

2. Respect Free Will: Respect the free will of others when engaging in financial magick. Avoid attempting to manipulate or control the decisions and actions of other people, as it goes against ethical principles. Focus on attracting opportunities and abundance rather than seeking to control external factors.

3. Avoid Manipulation: Do not use financial magick to deceive or manipulate financial outcomes. Instead, concentrate on improving your financial skills and mindset to attract genuine and sustainable prosperity.

4. Honesty and Transparency: Practice financial magick with honesty and transparency. Be truthful with yourself about your financial goals and intentions. Avoid self-deception or misrepresentation when setting financial targets.

5. Gratitude and Sharing: Cultivate a sense of gratitude for the financial blessings in your life and share your abundance with others. Act with generosity and support causes that promote financial well-being for all.

6. Karmic Awareness: Be aware of the karmic implications of your financial magick. Avoid engaging in unethical practices that could lead to negative karmic consequences. Instead, choose actions that contribute positively to your financial journey and the well-being of others.

7. Ethical Business Practices: If you are involved in business or entrepreneurship, ensure that your financial practices align with ethical standards. Uphold integrity in all financial transactions and dealings with clients, partners, and employees.

8. Give Back to the Community: Use your financial prosperity to support and give back to your community. Engage in philanthropic activities and contribute to initiatives that promote social and financial well-being for all.

Conclusion:

Ethical considerations are crucial when incorporating financial magick into your life. By aligning your financial practices with principles of integrity, respect, and compassion, you create a harmonious and positive financial journey.

8.6: The Magickal Abundance Blueprint for a Million-Dollar Reality

As we reach the pinnacle of our magickal journey to financial abundance, we find ourselves at the intersection of practical prosperity tips and the quest for making a million dollars. Within the realm of this magickal abundance blueprint, we uncover the keys that unlock the million-dollar reality we seek.

Affirmations for financial abundance become the sacred mantras that reprogram our subconscious mind for wealth and success. By reciting empowering affirmations daily, we align our thoughts with the million-dollar vibration, attracting opportunities and possibilities that resonate with our desires.

Gratitude practice becomes the transformative ritual that fosters wealth consciousness. As we cultivate an attitude of gratitude, we open ourselves to receive the abundance that the universe bestows upon us, acknowledging every step towards our million-dollar dreams.

Money magick in daily life becomes the integrated approach to financial success. We infuse our everyday activities with magickal intent, knowing that each action aligns us with the path of abundance and bridges the gap between where we are and where we wish to be financially.

Financial empowerment through budgeting and planning becomes the strategic foundation of our million-dollar journey. By meticulously managing our finances and setting clear goals, we steer the course towards prosperity, making informed decisions that pave the way to financial freedom.

Embracing ethical considerations becomes the moral compass that guides our magickal pursuits. As we embark on the quest to make a million dollars, we remain mindful of our impact on others and the world, ensuring that our actions are aligned with the greater good.

In this magickal abundance blueprint, we combine the wisdom of practical prosperity tips with the power of intention and belief. We understand that the journey to making a million dollars is not solely about material gain, but about personal growth, self-empowerment, and creating a positive impact in our lives and the lives of others.

As we wield this magickal abundance blueprint, we become the architects of our own destiny. With each affirmation uttered, with each expression of gratitude, with each magickal action taken, we pave the way towards the million-dollar reality we envision.

But amidst this grand design, we must remember that the true magick lies within ourselves. The universe responds to our belief, intention, and effort. As we immerse ourselves in the magickal abundance blueprint, we recognize that we are the catalysts for our own financial transformation.

As we journey through this chapter of our magickal quest, we stand on the threshold of the million-dollar reality that awaits. With the blueprint as our guide and the universe as our ally, we embrace the magickal potential that lies within and around us.

May this magickal abundance blueprint lead us towards a million-dollar destiny. As we integrate the wisdom of practical prosperity tips with the power of magickal intention, may we manifest our dreams of financial abundance and create a legacy that impacts generations to come.

As we step boldly into this magickal reality, may the million-dollar potential that resides within us be unleashed, and may the universe conspire to bring forth the wealth, success, and prosperity that are rightfully ours. Embrace the magick, and let the million-dollar journey begin!

8.7: Practical Exercises for Chapter 8

Exercise 1: Million-Dollar Affirmation Meditation

Use the power of affirmations to reprogram your subconscious mind for financial success and attract a million dollars with magick.

Instructions:

1. Find a quiet and comfortable space where you won't be disturbed.

2. Sit or lie down in a relaxed position.

3. Take a few deep breaths to center yourself and clear your mind.

4. Repeat a million-dollar affirmation of your choice. For example: "I am a magnet for a million dollars. Wealth and abundance flow effortlessly into my life."

5. As you repeat the affirmation, visualize yourself already living with a million dollars, feeling the excitement, joy, and gratitude that come with financial abundance.

6. Imagine how your life has transformed with the million dollars – the experiences you can afford, the freedom it brings, and the impact you can make.

7. Engage all your senses in this visualization, making it as vivid and real as possible.

8. Stay in this meditative state for at least 10-15 minutes, continuously affirming your million-dollar intention and maintaining a positive emotional state.

9. When you are ready to conclude the meditation, express gratitude for the manifestation of your million-dollar goal.

10. Practice this meditation daily or as often as you can to reinforce your positive beliefs and attract financial abundance.

Exercise 2: Gratitude Journal for Financial Abundance

Cultivate an attitude of gratitude and magnetize your path to making a million dollars with magick by keeping a gratitude journal.

Instructions:

1. Obtain a journal or notebook dedicated solely to this gratitude practice.

2. Set aside a few minutes each day to reflect on your financial journey and accomplishments.

3. Write down at least five things you are grateful for in relation to your finances. These can include past successes, present opportunities, or even future financial manifestations.

4. Express genuine gratitude for the money you already have and the progress you've made towards your million-dollar goal.

5. Along with material wealth, focus on non-material aspects like supportive relationships, personal growth, and the resources available to you.

6. When facing financial challenges, find aspects to be grateful for, even in difficult circumstances. This shift in perspective can open new avenues for solutions.

7. Read your gratitude journal entries regularly, especially during moments of doubt or uncertainty, to remind yourself of the abundance that surrounds you.

Exercise 3: Money Magick in Daily Actions

Infuse your daily actions with money magick by aligning them with your million-dollar intention and embracing opportunities for financial growth.

Instructions:

1. Set aside time each morning to review your financial goals and affirm your million-dollar intention.

2. Before engaging in financial tasks, such as budgeting or investing, light a green or gold candle and ask for magickal assistance in making wise decisions.

3. Incorporate money magick symbols into your daily life, such as carrying a green aventurine crystal in your wallet or placing a sigil of financial abundance on your desk.

4. When spending money, do so mindfully and with intention. Visualize the energy of prosperity flowing through your transactions.

5. Seek out opportunities for financial growth, whether through new investments, business ventures, or career advancements. Trust your intuition and magickal guidance in making decisions.

6. Embrace a mindset of abundance and generosity. Practice acts of kindness related to money, such as donating to charitable causes or supporting others on their financial journey.

7. Throughout the day, take moments to affirm your million-dollar intention silently or aloud, reinforcing your focus on attracting financial abundance.

8. Before going to bed, take a few moments to express gratitude for the financial opportunities and successes you experienced during the day.

Remember, making a million dollars with magick is a journey that combines intention, action, and belief in your own power. Practice these exercises consistently and trust in the magickal energies to support your financial goals. Good luck on your path to financial abundance and making a million dollars!

Chapter 8 Conclusion:

In the journey through practical prosperity tips, we have explored a variety of magickal practices and empowering strategies to enhance our financial well-being. Each tip serves as a powerful tool to align our thoughts, actions, and intentions with the flow of abundance in our lives.

From the potency of affirmations and the transformation of gratitude to the empowerment of budgeting and ethical considerations, these practical tips provide a comprehensive guide to fostering financial prosperity and success.

By embracing the magick of intention, visualization, and lunar cycles, we unlock the potential to manifest financial goals and attract abundance effortlessly. Through the elemental foundations of financial magick, we ground our intentions, gain clarity, and ignite the passion for financial growth.

The integration of crystals, tools of magick, and astrological influences empowers us to align our energies with the universal flow of abundance and tap into our innate power to create wealth.

As we infuse our daily lives with money magick, ethical principles guide us to act responsibly and harmoniously with the world around us. By respecting free will, avoiding manipulation, and practicing gratitude, we ensure that our financial journey is one of integrity and fairness.

May the exploration of practical prosperity tips empower you to embrace your magickal journey to financial abundance. Embrace the power of these tips as a means of aligning your thoughts, actions, and intentions with the flow of prosperity in your life. Trust in the energy of practical prosperity tips and the universe's response as you continue your journey towards financial success with confidence and grace.

May you thrive in financial abundance, harnessing the magick within to create a life of prosperity and fulfillment. As you walk the path of practical prosperity, may you find joy in the journey and embrace the magickal dance of financial abundance with open arms.

Chapter 9: Magick Spells to Make a Million Dollars

Spell 1: Million-Dollar Prosperity Enchantment

Ingredients:

A green pillar candle

A lodestone or pyrite crystal

A small piece of paper

Green ink or marker

A small pouch or fabric bag

Instructions:

1. Begin this spell on a Thursday, the day associated with wealth and abundance.

2. Light the green pillar candle and sit comfortably in front of it. Take a few deep breaths to center yourself and focus your mind on your million-dollar goal.

3. Take the piece of paper and write down your financial intention in green ink or marker. Be specific about the amount you wish to manifest, and use positive language, such as "I attract one million dollars with ease and grace."

4. Hold the lodestone or pyrite crystal in your hands and visualize it as a powerful magnet, drawing money and opportunities towards you.

5. Place the paper with your intention in front of the candle and position the lodestone or pyrite on top of it. As you do so, visualize the candle's flame and the crystal's energy amplifying your intention and attracting abundance.

6. Say the following incantation aloud three times: "Money flows to me, a million I see, With magick's might, my dreams take flight. As the candle glows, prosperity grows, Manifest my desire, with the universe's fire."

7. Fold the paper with your intention and the lodestone or pyrite inside it. Place the folded paper in the small pouch or fabric bag, and carry it with you daily as a talisman of prosperity.

8. Let the green pillar candle burn out completely. As it does, visualize your million-dollar intention becoming a reality.

Spell 2: Million-Dollar Money Jar

Ingredients:

A large glass jar with a lid

Green, gold, and silver ribbons

Fake or real dollar bills

Citrine or green aventurine crystals

Instructions:

1. Decorate the large glass jar with green, gold, and silver ribbons, representing prosperity, wealth, and financial success.

2. Fill the jar with fake or real dollar bills. If using fake bills, write your million-dollar goal on them with a gold marker.

3. Add citrine or green aventurine crystals to the jar. These stones symbolize abundance and amplify your financial intentions.

4. Close the lid of the jar tightly, sealing the energy within.

5. Hold the jar in your hands and visualize it as a powerful container of wealth and manifestation. Envision your million-dollar goal as if it has already been achieved.

6. Place the jar in a prominent area of your home, such as your living room or home office. Allow it to serve as a magickal reminder of your financial aspirations.

7. Each day, spend a few minutes in front of the jar, visualizing the money inside growing and multiplying. Feel gratitude for the abundance yet to come.

8. Add more dollar bills or replace the fake bills with real ones as you make progress toward your million-dollar goal.

Spell 3: Million-Dollar Prosperity Potion

Ingredients:

1 cup of purified water

A pinch of cinnamon

A pinch of nutmeg

A pinch of ginger

A pinch of cloves

3 coins (real or fake)

Instructions:

1. Begin this spell during a Waxing Moon phase, as it symbolizes growth and manifestation.

2. In a small cauldron or pot, combine the purified water, cinnamon, nutmeg, ginger, and cloves.

3. Place the cauldron on a heat-resistant surface and light a green or gold candle nearby to set the magickal ambiance.

4. As the water begins to warm, stir the ingredients clockwise three times with a wooden spoon, infusing them with your intention to make a million dollars.

5. Take the three coins and hold them between your palms. Close your eyes and visualize each coin multiplying into a million dollars. Feel the excitement and gratitude as your financial abundance grows.

6. Drop the coins into the cauldron with the infused water and spices. Continue to stir the potion clockwise while reciting the following incantation: "Water, fire, earth, and air, Multiply my wealth with care. From three coins to millions grand, I hold prosperity in my hand."

7. Allow the potion to simmer gently for a few minutes. As it cools, continue to infuse it with your million-dollar intention.

8. Once the potion is ready, strain it into a glass container, removing the spices and coins. Use the potion to anoint your wallet or sprinkle it around your home's entryway to invite financial prosperity.

Spell 4: Million-Dollar Abundance Talisman

Ingredients:

A green drawstring bag

A dollar bill (real or fake)

A green aventurine or citrine crystal

A small silver or gold charm representing money (e.g., a dollar sign or a gold bar)

Instructions:

1. Begin this spell during a Full Moon, as it is a powerful time for manifestation.

2. Place the dollar bill, green aventurine or citrine crystal, and the money charm inside the green drawstring bag.

3. Hold the bag in your hands and close your eyes. Visualize the bag filling with golden light and see your financial goal of making a million dollars coming true.

4. Whisper your million-dollar intention into the bag, infusing it with your desires for financial abundance.

5. Tie the drawstring bag shut, sealing the energy within. Keep the bag in a sacred space, such as your altar or bedside table.

6. Each day, take a moment to hold the talisman in your hands and reaffirm your intention to make a million dollars.

7. Carry the talisman with you whenever you engage in financial matters or important opportunities, knowing it acts as a powerful magnet for prosperity.

8. Trust that the talisman aligns your energy with the universe's abundant flow, bringing you one step closer to making a million dollars.

Spell 5: Million-Dollar Money Tree Manifestation

Ingredients:

A small potted plant (preferably a money tree or a plant associated with wealth)

A green ribbon

A dollar bill (real or fake)

A gold pen

Instructions:

1. Choose a potted plant that represents financial abundance, such as a money tree or a jade plant. Place it in a location where it will receive plenty of sunlight and positive energy.

2. Take the green ribbon and tie it around the base of the plant, symbolizing the growth of your financial wealth.

3. Using the gold pen, write your million-dollar intention on the dollar bill. Be specific and clear about the amount and the timeline for manifestation.

4. Fold the dollar bill neatly and tuck it into the soil of the potted plant. As you do so, visualize your intention being absorbed by the plant, just like water and nutrients nourish its growth.

5. Sit in front of the plant and close your eyes. Take several deep breaths and imagine yourself surrounded by a golden light of abundance. Feel the energy of prosperity flowing through you.

6. Speak your intention aloud with conviction, affirming that you are worthy and capable of making a million dollars.

7. Water the plant, pouring the water with intention and gratitude for the financial abundance you are manifesting.

8. Care for the plant regularly, nurturing it with love and attention. Each time you tend to the plant, reaffirm your intention and visualize your million-dollar goal coming to fruition.

Spell 6: Million-Dollar Money Shower

Ingredients:

A gold or green shower curtain

A waterproof marker or gold paint pen

A small spray bottle filled with water

A small green or gold charm (e.g., a dollar sign or a gemstone)

Instructions:

1. Hang the gold or green shower curtain in your bathroom, symbolizing the shower of wealth and prosperity coming into your life.

2. With the waterproof marker or gold paint pen, write your million-dollar intention directly on the shower curtain. You may write phrases like "I attract a million dollars" or "Financial abundance flows to me effortlessly."

3. Keep the small spray bottle filled with water nearby. Before taking a shower, hold the spray bottle in your hands and infuse it with your million-dollar intention. Visualize the water as a potent magickal tool for attracting financial abundance.

4. Step into the shower and close your eyes. Imagine that each droplet of water falling on you is charged with the energy of wealth and prosperity.

5. Repeat your million-dollar intention out loud as you shower. Feel the water cleansing away any financial blocks or limitations, making way for the manifestation of your goal.

6. After your shower, stand in front of the shower curtain and place the small green or gold charm on it. This charm acts as a symbol of your intention and serves as a constant reminder of your million-dollar magick.

7. Take a few moments to express gratitude for the abundance that is on its way to you. Trust that the universe is aligning with your intentions to bring forth financial success.

8. Continue to use the Million-Dollar Money Shower regularly, knowing that your daily shower has become a powerful ritual for attracting wealth and prosperity.

Spell 7: Million-Dollar Prosperity Pathway

Ingredients:

A green or gold ribbon (long enough to create a pathway)

Green or gold stones (such as aventurine, jade, or citrine)

A small bowl of soil

A green or gold candle

A small green or gold charm (optional)

Instructions:

1. Choose a quiet and undisturbed space outdoors, like your garden or a secluded spot in nature, to perform this spell.

2. Lay the green or gold ribbon on the ground, creating a pathway leading towards your chosen space.

3. Along the pathway, place the green or gold stones, infusing them with your intention for financial prosperity. Visualize each stone representing a stepping stone towards your million-dollar goal.

4. Set the small bowl of soil at the end of the pathway. This bowl symbolizes the fertile ground of opportunity and manifestation.

5. Light the green or gold candle near the bowl of soil, illuminating the pathway. As you do so, imagine the candle's flame as the guiding light to your financial success.

6. Stand at the beginning of the pathway and take a few deep breaths, grounding yourself in the present moment.

7. Begin walking along the pathway, stepping on each stone with purpose and determination. As you walk, affirm your intention to make a million dollars with each step.

8. When you reach the end of the pathway, hold your hands over the bowl of soil, channeling your energy into it. Speak your million-dollar intention aloud, declaring that your dreams are coming to fruition.

9. If you have a small green or gold charm, bury it in the soil as a symbol of your financial desires taking root and growing.

10. Close the spell by expressing gratitude for the universe's support in manifesting your million-dollar goal. Leave the candle burning until it naturally extinguishes.

Spell 8: Million-Dollar Prosperity Blessing

Ingredients:

A green or gold envelope

A blank piece of paper

A green or gold ink pen

A green or gold ribbon

A dollar bill (real or fake)

Instructions:

1. Sit in a quiet and serene space where you can focus without distractions.

2. Take the blank piece of paper and write your million-dollar intention in green or gold ink. Be specific and detailed about how you plan to achieve your financial goal.

3. Fold the paper neatly and place it inside the green or gold envelope. Seal the envelope with the ribbon, symbolizing the containment of your million-dollar desires.

4. Hold the envelope in your hands and close your eyes. Take several deep breaths, allowing yourself to feel centered and connected to your intention.

5. With the envelope still in your hands, visualize a golden light enveloping it, infusing it with the energy of abundance and prosperity.

6. Place the dollar bill inside the envelope along with the intention paper. This dollar bill represents the first step towards your million-dollar goal.

7. Seal the envelope securely and hold it to your heart. Speak your million-dollar intention aloud with conviction, believing in your power to make it happen.

8. Find a special place to keep the envelope, such as a treasure box or a sacred space on your altar. Revisit it regularly, focusing on your intention and reaffirming your commitment to achieving financial success.

9. As you go about your daily activities, trust that the universe is aligning with your intention and that opportunities for financial abundance are coming your way.

10. Open the envelope when your million-dollar goal has been achieved, celebrating your magickal journey to prosperity.

Spell 9: Million-Dollar Prosperity Mirror

Ingredients:

A small mirror with a gold or green frame

A green or gold cloth

A gold or green candle

A small piece of paper

A gold or green ink pen

Instructions:

1. Begin this spell during a Waxing Crescent Moon, as it symbolizes growth and potential.

2. Place the green or gold cloth on a flat surface, such as your altar or a clean table.

3. Set the small mirror on top of the cloth, with the reflective side facing up. This mirror represents the portal to your million-dollar reality.

4. Light the gold or green candle near the mirror, allowing its flame to reflect and dance on the surface.

5. Take the piece of paper and write your million-dollar intention in gold or green ink. Be specific, describing the financial success you desire and the impact it will have on your life.

6. Hold the paper in front of the mirror, gazing at your reflection. Visualize yourself in a future moment of financial achievement, already enjoying the abundance of making a million dollars.

7. Affirm your intention out loud with conviction, stating it as if it has already come to pass. For example, say, "I am grateful for making a million dollars and the opportunities it brings."

8. Place the intention paper next to the lit candle and the mirror, ensuring it is in your view when looking into the mirror.

9. Sit in front of the mirror and observe your reflection. Envision yourself surrounded by a golden aura of prosperity and success.

10. Close your eyes and meditate for a few moments, feeling the energy of your million-dollar intention vibrating through every cell of your being.

11. Blow out the candle, signifying the end of the ritual. As you do so, know that your intention is now activated and aligned with the universe's abundant flow.

12. Keep the mirror in a sacred space or on your altar, and each day, take a moment to connect with it and visualize your financial dreams as already fulfilled.

Spell 10: Million-Dollar Pathway of Coins

Ingredients:

Real or fake coins (gold or silver, your choice)

A green or gold cloth

A small bag or pouch (green or gold)

A gold or green ribbon

Instructions:

1. Find a quiet and secluded outdoor area, preferably a park or natural setting where you can lay out the coins undisturbed.

2. Lay the green or gold cloth on the ground, creating a pathway.

3. Place the coins along the pathway, spacing them out evenly. As you do so, visualize each coin as a stepping stone towards your million-dollar goal.

4. Sit at the beginning of the pathway and hold the small bag or pouch in your hands. This bag will become a talisman of your financial manifestation.

5. Speak your million-dollar intention aloud, declaring your intention to make a million dollars and inviting financial success into your life.

6. Walk along the pathway, stepping on each coin with purpose and intention. As you walk, envision yourself moving confidently towards financial abundance.

7. Once you reach the end of the pathway, pick up each coin one by one and place them into the small bag or pouch.

8. Tie the bag shut with the gold or green ribbon, sealing the energy of your million-dollar intention.

9. Carry the bag with you as a talisman of prosperity, reminding yourself of your financial goal and the actions you are taking to achieve it.

10. Each time you hold the bag, visualize the coins multiplying and growing into a million dollars, feeling gratitude for the abundance yet to come.

Spell 11: Million-Dollar Money Jar Manifestation

Ingredients:

A large glass jar with a green or gold lid

A green or gold ribbon

A green or gold candle

Green or gold paper (cut into small pieces)

A pen with green or gold ink

A citrine or pyrite crystal

Instructions:

1. Choose a quiet and sacred space to perform this spell, preferably near your altar or a peaceful corner of your home.

2. Place the large glass jar in the center of your chosen space.

3. Light the green or gold candle near the jar, infusing the area with the energy of prosperity.

4. Take the small pieces of green or gold paper and write on each one a specific way you will make money or attract financial opportunities. Examples include "Start a successful business," "Receive a promotion at work," "Win a profitable investment," etc.

5. Fold each paper neatly and place them inside the jar, one by one, creating a powerful collection of your million-dollar intentions.

6. Hold the citrine or pyrite crystal in your hands and infuse it with your financial goals. Visualize it amplifying your intentions and attracting abundant opportunities.

7. Place the crystal into the jar, allowing it to charge the papers with its powerful energy.

8. Close the jar with the green or gold lid, symbolizing the containment of your million-dollar manifestations.

9. Tie the green or gold ribbon around the jar, sealing it with a magickal touch.

10. Set the jar on your altar or a prominent place where you will see it daily. Whenever you pass by, take a moment to hold the jar and visualize your intentions coming to fruition.

11. On the New Moon, Full Moon, and any significant financial dates, light the green or gold candle near the jar and reaffirm your million-dollar intentions.

12. As opportunities arise, or you take inspired actions towards your financial goals, write them on new pieces of green or gold paper and add them to the jar, continually empowering your manifestation.

Spell 12: Million-Dollar Affirmation Mirror

Ingredients:

A small handheld mirror with a green or gold frame

Green or gold stickers or markers

A green or gold cloth

Instructions:

1. Choose a quiet and comfortable space where you can focus without distractions.

2. Place the green or gold cloth on the ground or table, creating a sacred space for your mirror spell.

3. Hold the mirror in your hands and gaze at your reflection. Take a few deep breaths, centering yourself in the present moment.

4. Decorate the mirror frame with green or gold stickers or markers, symbolizing your intention to attract financial abundance.

5. Look into the mirror and affirm your million-dollar goal out loud. For example, say, "I am a magnet for a million dollars, and it flows effortlessly into my life."

6. Close your eyes and visualize yourself already in possession of the million dollars you desire. Feel the excitement and gratitude as if it were already a reality.

7. Open your eyes and look into the mirror again, this time repeating your affirmation with even more conviction.

8. Hold the mirror close to your heart and express gratitude for the universe's support in manifesting your financial dreams.

9. Place the mirror in a prominent location, such as your bedroom or altar. Each morning and night, look into the mirror and repeat your million-dollar affirmation, feeling the energy of abundance flowing through you.

10. Trust that the mirror is a powerful tool to reflect your intentions back to you, assisting you on your journey to making a million dollars.

Spell 13: Rapid Million-Dollar Manifestation Candle

Ingredients:

A green or gold pillar candle

A pen with green or gold ink

A piece of paper

A green or gold ribbon

Instructions:

1. Begin this spell during a Waxing Gibbous Moon, as it symbolizes increasing power and amplification.

2. Sit in a quiet and undisturbed space, holding the green or gold candle in your hands.

3. Use the pen with green or gold ink to write your million-dollar intention on the piece of paper. Be bold and specific, expressing your desire to make a million dollars quickly and easily.

4. Roll up the paper tightly and tie it with the green or gold ribbon, symbolizing the swift manifestation of your financial goal.

5. Light the green or gold candle, infusing it with the energy of rapid financial success.

6. Hold the paper in front of the lit candle, allowing the flame to engulf your intention with its energy.

7. Speak your million-dollar intention aloud, stating it with unwavering confidence and certainty.

8. Place the paper near the candle and let it burn, visualizing the flames carrying your intention to the universe with incredible speed.

9. Close your eyes and meditate for a few moments, feeling the energy of financial abundance flowing to you effortlessly.

10. Keep the tied paper as a powerful talisman, and whenever you need a boost of manifestation energy, hold it in your hands, repeating your intention with faith and determination.

Spell 14: Million-Dollar Prosperity Amulet

Ingredients:

A green or gold drawstring pouch

Green or gold gemstones (such as emerald, peridot, or goldstone)

A piece of paper

A pen with green or gold ink

Instructions:

1. Find a peaceful space to perform this spell, preferably near your altar or a place of personal significance.

2. Take the green or gold drawstring pouch in your hands and hold it close to your heart, setting the intention to make a million dollars quickly.

3. Place the green or gold gemstones inside the pouch, charging them with your million-dollar intention. Visualize them radiating with abundance and prosperity.

4. On the piece of paper, write your million-dollar goal using green or gold ink. Be concise and affirmative, declaring your financial success.

5. Fold the paper and place it inside the pouch, alongside the gemstones, to enhance the amulet's power.

6. Close the pouch with the drawstring, sealing your intention securely within it.

7. Hold the amulet in your hands and infuse it with your energy, repeating your million-dollar affirmation out loud.

8. Carry the amulet with you as a powerful magnet for financial abundance, feeling its energy attracting opportunities and prosperity.

9. Keep the amulet close to you, either in your pocket, purse, or under your pillow, to stay connected to its magickal energy.

10. Recharge the amulet with your intention regularly, repeating the spell on the Full Moon for added potency.

Spell 15: Million-Dollar Money Magnet Bath

Ingredients:

A green or gold candle

Green or gold bath salts or essential oils

A small piece of paper

A pen with green or gold ink

Instructions:

1. Prepare a warm bath, infusing it with green or gold bath salts or essential oils. This ritual bath represents a cleansing of old financial limitations and an invitation for prosperity.

2. Light the green or gold candle near the bathtub, creating a soothing ambiance for your spell.

3. Write your million-dollar intention on the piece of paper using green or gold ink. Be clear and positive in your wording.

4. Place the paper near the candle, allowing the warm glow to illuminate your intention.

5. Step into the bath and immerse yourself fully, feeling the water enveloping your body with a sense of renewal and empowerment.

6. Take the piece of paper and submerge it in the bathwater, allowing your intention to merge with the water's energy.

7. Close your eyes and visualize your million-dollar goal coming to fruition rapidly, feeling the excitement and joy of your financial success.

8. As you soak in the bath, repeat your million-dollar affirmation out loud, reinforcing your intention.

9. After the bath, let the paper dry, then keep it in a special place, such as your altar or a sacred box, to preserve its magickal energy.

10. Continue this bath ritual regularly, allowing the energy of the water and your million-dollar intention to manifest your financial desires with incredible speed.

Remember, while magick can be a powerful ally in manifesting your desires, it works best when combined with proactive actions and a positive mindset. May these spells empower you on your quest to make a million dollars, and may the universe align with your intentions, bringing you swift and abundant financial success.

Conclusion: Embrace the Magickal Million-Dollar Destiny

As we reach the culmination of this magickal journey, we stand at the precipice of a new reality—one where the manifestation of a million-dollar fortune is within your grasp. Throughout the pages of "Make a Million Dollars with Magick," we have explored the arcane wisdom, rituals, and practices that bridge the mystical and the material, guiding you towards the pinnacle of financial abundance.

Embrace the truth that you are a powerful creator of your own destiny. Armed with the potent tools of intention, visualization, and universal energy, you possess the magickal ability to attract wealth and prosperity beyond measure.

Harness the elemental forces, the dance of the planets, and the ethereal lunar cycles, for they conspire to align the universe in your favor. As you weave the threads of crystals, talismans, and prosperity spells into the tapestry of your financial journey, know that you are activating the hidden keys to the vault of abundance.

But remember, dear seeker of magick, that with great power comes great responsibility. Embrace ethical considerations as the guiding compass on your path to a million-dollar destiny. Align your intentions with integrity and fairness, and let the spirit of giving back to the world infuse your financial ventures with purpose and compassion.

As you move forward, never lose sight of your dreams, for they are the fuel that ignites the flames of your success. Cultivate unwavering faith, belief, and a heart full of gratitude, for these are the magickal ingredients that transmute dreams into reality.

The journey to a million-dollar fortune is not without challenges, but remember that every obstacle is an opportunity for growth. Stay steadfast in your commitment, and with the resilience of a magickal practitioner, transform setbacks into stepping stones towards greatness.

With the turning of each page, you have delved deeper into the realm of magick, unlocking the secrets that transcend the ordinary and reveal the extraordinary within. Your million-dollar destiny awaits, ready to unfold in all its grandeur.

As the final words of this magickal tome embrace you, let them echo in your heart as a reminder of your innate power. For you, dear reader, are the alchemist of your own fate, and the magick of making a million dollars lies within your soul.

Embrace the magickal million-dollar destiny that beckons you. The universe conspires to fulfill your desires, and the million-dollar fortune awaits those who dare to believe. With the spark of magick and the flame of determination, let your journey to financial abundance begin.

You are the magick, and the magick is you. Embrace it, wield it, and make a million dollars with magick. The stars align, the elements converge, and the universe celebrates your ascent to prosperity.

The time has come to embrace your magickal destiny. The time has come to make a million dollars with magick.

Are you ready to claim what is rightfully yours? The universe whispers its answer—a resounding yes. Let the magick unfold.

Don't miss out!

Visit the website below and you can sign up to receive emails whenever Anjelica Shaw publishes a new book. There's no charge and no obligation.

https://books2read.com/r/B-A-IFWZ-NVOMC

BOOKS 2 READ

Connecting independent readers to independent writers.

Milton Keynes UK
Ingram Content Group UK Ltd.
UKHW021839240823
427419UK00016B/483